The World of Flora Thompson

Frontispiece: Flora Thompson
(Henry Westbury)

The World of Flora Thompson

Christine Bloxham

Robert Dugdale, Oxford
1998

First published in 1998 by Robert Dugdale, Oxford
and distributed from 26 Norham Road, Oxford ox2 6sf

ISBN 0 946978 06 6

Designed and typeset in Monotype Bulmer by Paul Cleal
Printed by The Alden Press, Oxford and Northampton

CONTENTS

ACKNOWLEDGEMENTS

Many people have generously given help and information in the writing of this book. My thanks go above all to David Watts, without whom this book would have been a great deal slimmer, who has generously offered his vast expertise and information on the Oxfordshire area, done additional research, and generously contributed much on the Wallington family, collated most of the family trees, and lent local photographs. His father, John Watts, generously gave me access to unpublished material and photographs, James and Audrey Lambert gave information on the Waine family history, William and Beryl Plumb and Miss Agnes Plumb gave fascinating information about the forge at Fringford. Henry Westbury generously let me have access to unpublished letters Flora Thompson wrote to her nephew Leslie Castle and family photographs. Elizabeth Swaffield gave me permission to use unpublished material now housed in the Harry Ransom Humanities Research Centre at the University of Texas at Austin. David Morris and his wife, who kept the Fox Inn at Juniper Hill for many years have generously allowed me access to unpublished information about Juniper Hill and the use of photographs. Baroness von Maltzahn also kindly let me use several photographs. The late Patrick Kirkby gave me access to his researches and much encouragement.

Oxford University Press kindly gave permission to quote from *Lark Rise to Candleford* (the page numbers refer to the edition published by Penguin Books), from *Still Glides the Stream*, and from *A Country Calendar and other writings*. The page numbers attached to *Heatherley* refer to the pages of *A Country Calendar*, which also includes some of Flora's poetry, and a selection of her nature writings. More of these writings have been published in *The Peverel Papers*, edited by Julian Shuckburgh and published by Century Hutchinson, who have kindly authorised quotations from them. John Murray (Publishers) Ltd gave permission for Joan Hassall's drawings of Juniper Hill and Cottisford Church, first published in Margaret Lane, *Flora Thompson*, 1977, to be reproduced in the book (pp. 6 and 232).

Gillian Lindsay, author of *Flora Thompson, The Lark Rise Writer*, generously shared her expertise, and Anne Mallinson gave invaluable help about Flora's time in the Liphook area. Jo Smith gave advice on Grayshott and let me read his plays about Flora. Kathleen Hunt gave much interesting local information and access to family photographs, while Madeleine Bennett gave valuable information about and checked the chapter on Ardley and Fewcott. Many local people gave information, including Flora's nephew Bernard Lane, Rev. Ricky Yates, Mr and Mrs Winnington Ingram, Baroness von Maltzahn, Mr and Mrs Bell and Simon and Vanda Emery (who are descended from Uncle Tom and revealed his real identity). Susanne Shatford helped with work on the Timms and Lapper family trees.

My thanks go also to the librarians in Oxford and Winchester and at the *Bicester Advertiser* and the Harry Ransom Humanities Research Centre at the University of Texas at Austin. I am infinitely grateful to my father, John Bloxham, for drawing a diagram, to my husband, Norman Blanks, who has taken on many extra tasks while I have been writing the book, including proof-reading, and my sons, Richard and Peter, and to Hugo Brunner, my publisher who has let me expand the book way beyond the original brief and been very patient with me.

1887 Ordnance Survey map showing the area where Flora was brought up. Banbury, one of the towns she visited, is about ten miles to the West of Brackley and Pidding-ton, where her grandmother Martha Wallington was born, is south east of Bicester. (Centre for Oxfordshire Studies)

Introduction

᭰

Flora Thompson once met an ancient gypsy woman when she was wandering in the woods, and was rewarded for helping her find medicinal wood-sage by having her fortune read:

> "... to thank me she promised me all the delightful happenings she could lay tongue to. No, not quite all; there was no dark or fair stranger. Neither did she promise me riches: she passed such things over disdainfully, as stock properties kept for the commonalty who crossed her hand with a shilling. She even confided that she did not go by the hand at all, that it was only a formality to secure the shilling.
>
> 'It's the face,' she said, 'not the hand. It's all writ in the face what a person is. And if I know what you are, I can tell pretty well how things'll go with you!'
>
> She was certainly able to read the secret desire, for she promised me love and praise and friendship!
>
> 'You are goin' to be loved,' she said, 'loved by a lot o' folks— strangers shall become friends—people all over—' and she waved her bundle of wood-sage to include the entire horizon.
>
> Nonsense, of course. Yet after I parted from her, I trod more lightly, and strange to say, when I reached home I found a letter awaiting me from a complete stranger praising some trifle I had written."

Flora Thompson, from *The Peverel Papers* quoted in *A Country Calendar*, Oxford University Press 1979, page 131.

The gypsy's prophecy was made to Flora Thompson at a time long before the publication of her famous trilogy *Lark Rise to Candleford*, when she can

1

have had no inkling of how popular her work was to become, indeed she died just as her work was beginning to become well known. That her trilogy was written at all came as a great surprise to many who had known her. When the villagers of Juniper Hill heard that their Flora Timms had published a book, they were dumbfounded and racked their brains to recall the stonemason's daughter they had known as a child, (she had not lived in Juniper since she was fourteen, and had seldom visited it as an adult) and the only thing that came to mind about her was that she was good at skipping!

Flora Thompson, born Flora Jane Timms on 5 December 1876, was the daughter of Albert Timms, a stonemason, and his wife Emma who had been a nursemaid, who brought her up in the tiny village of Juniper Hill in North Oxfordshire. She was a quiet child, an observer rather than participator from a very early age, always noticeably different from the boisterous village children, who carefully noted in her mind details of the people and places around her. Most of the girls who were contemporary with her at school left to become servants, whereas she was lucky enough to find work in a post office and, by dint of reading as much as she could, succeeded in becoming a poet and writer, writing material as diverse as romantic short stories, nature notes and ghost-writing for a big-game hunter. She even had the confidence in her own abilities, and desire to help others in her own position, to found and successfully run a society (The Peverel Society) to encourage poets and give writing lessons. However she will be best remembered for her *pièces de résistance*, the trilogy *Lark Rise to Candleford* and *Still Glides the Stream*, books written in her later years, as she began to realise that people were interested in Victorian rural life, based very much on her memories of her childhood. A measure of her quality as a writer is that these were published by the Oxford University Press, which had to describe *Lark Rise to Candleford* as autobiography as they did not publish fiction, but were so impressed by Flora's writing that they were determined to publish it. Not only did they publish it, but Sir Humphrey Milford, the Publisher, gave her a great accolade when he wrote in the *Periodical*, the house magazine of the Oxford University Press, that he considered that the two most important books he had published during his 22 years at the Press were Arnold Toynbee's *A Study of History* and Flora Thompson's *Lark Rise to Candleford*.

Although her first publication, a slim volume of poetry entitled *Bog Myrtle and Peat*, has long been out of print, we are fortunate that a wide variety of Flora's work has been published since her death. Margaret Lane wrote a short biography of Flora and has edited various pieces including some of the nature notes she wrote for the *Catholic Fireside*, *Heatherley* (a continuation of her autobiography which covered her time at the post office in Grayshott) and some of her poems for a book entitled *A Country Calendar and other writings*. Julian Shuckburgh edited a longer version of her nature notes in *The Peverel Papers*, and Gillian Lindsay has skilfully researched a biography of Flora, *Flora Thompson, The Lark Rise Writer*, revealing much about her hitherto unknown later life. John Owen Smith has done detective work on her life at Grayshott and Liphook in *On the Trail of Flora Thompson beyond Candleford Green*

It was a great personal achievement for Flora to become such an accomplished writer. She came from an ordinary, relatively uneducated country background, which did not readily breed writers. Books about the working classes have generally been written by people of middle or even upper class status, who have not experienced the actual way of life themselves, but Flora was able to write from her own experience, giving an authoritative account of some of the hardships and pleasures of rural life at the end of the 19th century. Throughout her work one finds little asides, pointing out that for many it was a struggle to survive. She drew largely from her own rather restricted experience of life in small Oxfordshire villages for her writing, and because of this the same characters, such as her family and her neighbours Sally and Queenie, are found in several guises in different stories and articles, often written many years apart. The quality and detail of Flora's writing has made it a rich source for historians of Victorian rural life.

However, the material when used for this purpose, has to be treated with caution, because although *Lark Rise to Candleford* is a thinly veiled autobiography—for example, Flora changed the name of her heroine to 'Laura', and her brother Edwin's name to 'Edmund'—it must be remembered that she was writing many years after the events she describes, and used a certain amount of artistic licence, taking the basic characters and working her magic as a creative writer upon them. In some cases she deliberately disguised the names of people and places, perhaps to spare her family and her friends embarrassment. For example while she was writing *Still Glides the Stream*, a novel about retired school teacher Charity Finch recalling her rural childhood, she was sent a traditional rhyme about local church spires by her nephew Leslie Castle: "Adderbury for length, Bloxham for strength and Kings Sutton for beauty". She commented : "I want to use it to draw a red herring over the trail in the new book I am writing." (Quoted in a letter written to Leslie Castle in July 1946). However, careful detective work, looking at parish registers, census returns, maps and local documents and consulting surviving members of the family, has helped to identify some people and places, and enough pieces of the jig-saw can be found to fill out the background to the story.

Flora Thompson was deeply influenced by her background and the people and places she knew, and the aim of this book is to discover more about them, to reveal more about Flora and her work by setting it in its context. The book concentrates on her Oxfordshire background, which most touched her and was the main inspiration for all her writing apart from her nature notes.

Flora's world as a child was a very small, circumscribed one. She was born in the tiny hamlet of Juniper Hill, on the Oxfordshire/Northamptonshire border, and went to school in its mother village of Cottisford. Her first job was only a few miles away, working in the Post Office at Fringford. She visited relations in Buckingham and Twyford, and shopped in Brackley, where her father worked. She later wrote that she visited Banbury in the carrier's cart, and must have visited Bicester from Fringford. Although she loved the area, she knew little about the places beyond her immediate area, apparently never even visiting Ardley where her mother was born.

"I . . . have always wanted to go also to Ardley, where your Grandmother was born. I can imagine how lovely in its quiet way that part of

FLORA THOMPSON'S FAMILY TREE

*for further details see the Wallington, Timms,
and Dibber family trees*

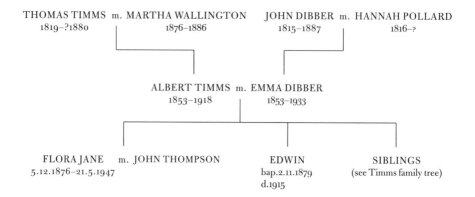

THOMAS TIMMS m. MARTHA WALLINGTON   JOHN DIBBER m. HANNAH POLLARD
1819–?1880   1876–1886   1815–1887   1816–?

ALBERT TIMMS m. EMMA DIBBER
1853–1918   1853–1933

FLORA JANE   m. JOHN THOMPSON   EDWIN   SIBLINGS
5.12.1876–21.5.1947   bap.2.11.1879   (see Timms family tree)
                                   d.1915

the country is now looking with the elder and the dog-roses out in the hedges and the crops coming on in the fields."

(Extract from a letter to her nephew Leslie Castle in July 1946)

In her later years she evinced a great interest in her family background, being conscious that on her father's side she had ancestors, the Wallingtons of Piddington, who had been of higher social status than her immediate family. She herself knew little about them, sending her nephew off on a wild goose chase to visit the Heyfords to see if he could find any family tombstones, when in fact the family did not come from those villages at all. She would have been fascinated to know about the real history of the Wallington family, which has recently come to light, and from which her paternal grandmother came.

1

Piddington—The Wallington Connection

⁊ᗝ

Flora scarcely mentions her paternal grandmother Martha Wallington in her books, although she visited her regularly in Buckingham until she was about ten, and was evidently a little in awe of her. She was, however, very significant to Flora in that it was through Martha that she could claim ancestry of higher standing than her own. Flora was not ashamed of her upbringing, but evidently felt it put her at a disadvantage in her writing: as a stonemason's daughter brought up in a small village she had not had a good education. In her early writing days she believed that if people knew who she really was they would not be interested in reading what she had to say, so she invented an imaginary persona as a doctor's daughter. She recalled her grandmother when writing to her nephew Leslie Castle in 1943:

"My grandmother . . . on my father's side, belonged to a good family described in my childhood as gentleman farmers and Aunt Jane . . . told me that when she was a child she was once taken on a visit to some branch of the family when she saw paintings and poems painted and written by one of the sons . . . I remember my grandmother distinctly as she did not die until I was eleven and we went every year to Buckingham to visit her. She was a woman of refinement and must have been recognised as such as her chief friend was a doctor in the town named King. She brought the brown eyes into the Timms family, so you can see something of her in your mother any day. She had some beautiful old china and other family things which, quite properly, went to the daughter who gave her a home and nursed her through her last illness. My father had some miniatures as part of his share of the family treasure after his mother died, but, unfortunately, there was nobody to appreciate them and they were destroyed by the children."

Flora would have talked to her father Albert Timms about her grandmother, as he was the one who instilled in her the pride in the their connection with the Wallington family. Some of the details he remembered about the Wallingtons were mythical, including the suggestion that they were related to General Sir John Wallington and his son who was secretary to Queen Mary, wife of King George V.

According to the family legend Martha had been '*a lady by birth*', an heiress, and had made a runaway match with Flora's grandfather Thomas Timms. One of the favourite family stories was that of 'Granny's golden footstool':

" Their father's parents had at one time kept a public-house and livery stables in Oxford and the story ran that, either going to, or coming from, the 'Horse and Rider', their grandfather had handed their grandmother into the carriage and placed a box containing a thousand pounds at her feet, saying: 'It's not every lady who can ride in her own carriage with a golden footstool.'

They must have been on their way there with the purchase money, for they can have brought no golden footstool away with them. Before that adventure, made possible by a legacy left to the grandmother by one of her relatives, the grandfather had been a builder in a small way, and, after it, he went back to building again, in a still smaller way, presumably, for by the time Laura was born the family business had disappeared and her father was working for wages."

Lark Rise to Candleford, p. 274.

The real story was far more fascinating than Flora realised. Certainly Martha was of higher birth—but more of yeoman stock than of the aristocracy, and, although the great fortune was a family myth, Martha had a traumatic childhood, details about which do not appear to have been common knowledge by Flora's time.

Martha Wallington was baptised on 2 June 1816 in the small village of Piddington, about five miles south of Bicester, which had only 427 inhabi-

1. The village school and and icicle-hung cottage in Piddington, *c*.1900 (John Watts)

tants in 1814. John Drinkwater described the village as it was in the 19th century, when the Wallingtons lived there:

> "It is a plain, grey little village, neutral in design, ambling from cottage to cottage with no apparent sense of direction, its half dozen larger houses of red brick sitting discreetly here and there at the roadside ... When I knew it a stranger was seen only when one passed through in the carrier's cart, or when the Irish labourers came over for harvest, a talkative, thirsty lot, sleeping in the lofts and barns. In the winter, when icicles were on the thatch eaves, the village would lie for days as if it were asleep."

> John Drinkwater, *Inheritance, being the first book of an autobiography*, p. 46

She was one of the children of Martha Shaw, who was born in 1784, daughter of John Shaw, a yeoman of Piddington, whose family had been in the village since about 1690. Martha married Edward Wallington in 1805. Edward, born in 1781, belonged to a family that had farmed in Ludgershall, Buckinghamshire since the late sixteenth century, but he came to Piddington to run his wife's farm on their marriage.

Their farmhouse was in the centre of the village at the road junction with Arncott Road, opposite the bakehouse. The house, which still stands today, is basically eighteenth century. It was built by John Shaw (1718–97), Martha's great–grandfather, whose initials I.S. 1777 are carved on the date-stone, though it incorporates earlier elements. He purchased much of the farm from Sir John Aubrey, fourth baronet of Llantrithyd. His son, John Shaw the Younger (1755–1800), died, leaving the farmhouse and farm in trust for his second wife Sarah Toms of Kidlington, and his only daughter, Martha (by his first marriage), who five years later married Edward Wallington. Their farm consisted of house and garden, orchard, barn, stables and yard, rickyard, cowhouse and yard, a paddock, pasture and arable land.

2. Brown's Piece, Piddington, the farmhouse built by Martha Wallington's great–grandfather, John Shaw, where she lived as a child. (David Watts)

Either the farm was not a very profitable one, or Edward was not very careful with money, because in 1805 Martha and Edward had to borrow £700 from her aunt Elizabeth Shaw (1751–1820) to buy farm stock, putting up their farm as security. It seems that the farm still did not prosper, as by 1815 the Wallingtons owed Elizabeth Shaw the vast sum of £1647 0s 0d, so by indenture made on 3 November the ownership of the farm passed to her in payment of the debt, with the proviso that the Wallingtons could have it back on repayment of the money and interest owing. When Elizabeth died in 1820 she left the farm to her niece Martha for her lifetime, and it was then to be equally shared among the Wallington children. She obviously had no time or respect for Edward Wallington, considering him a spendthrift, as he was to be kept from any responsibility running the farm and was to have no further personal interest in it should his wife die before him.

In 1824 tragedy struck the Wallingtons when some illness, possibly plague, according to family tradition, killed several of them within a few weeks: first children—Francis, aged 14, buried on 8 March, then Edwin aged six, buried on 21 March, then their mother Martha herself, aged 40, buried on 30 March. Then, when the family must have felt that everything was improving, John, aged 17, died and was buried on 17 May. A year later Martha's husband Edward, died aged only 44 and was buried on 6 March 1824. The five remaining children were left orphans: Edward, the eldest, was aged only 16, Elizabeth aged 13, Leonard, aged 12, Martha aged 8 and little Clementina aged 3. None of their near relatives seems to have wanted to take on responsibility for them, their two uncles claiming that they could not do so, being in 'indifferent circumstances' themselves. It is not clear what happened then, except that their father seems not to have left any money of his own, certainly not enough to pay off the debt he owed to the late Elizabeth Shaw to redeem the farm, but the provisions of Elizabeth's will to sell the farm and divide the money between the children were not carried out. The children seem to have gone on living in the house, when they were not at boarding school, but evidently the farm did not bring in enough money to keep them, so they ran up extensive bills with local tradesmen. Something had to be done to raise money, and the legal position was uncertain.

This parlous situation carried on for five years, but in 1829 Edward, the eldest surviving child, had reached his majority and needed money to marry Mary Sulston, so it was decided that the situation must be clarified. On 2 May the case was taken to the Court of Chancery where it was claimed that on Martha's death the provisions of Elizabeth Shaw's will had not been

THE WALLINGTON FAMILY

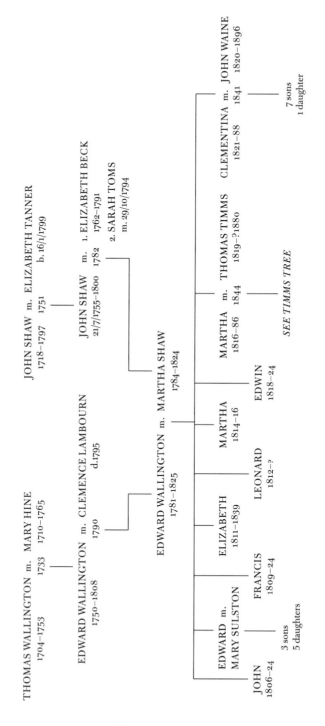

THOMAS WALLINGTON m. MARY HINE
1704–1753   1733   1710–1765

JOHN SHAW m. ELIZABETH TANNER
1718–1797   1751   b. 16/1/1799

EDWARD WALLINGTON m. CLEMENCE LAMBOURN
1750–1808   1790   d.1795

JOHN SHAW m. 1. ELIZABETH BECK
21/7/1755–1800   1782   1762–1791
2. SARAH TOMS
m. 29/10/1794

EDWARD WALLINGTON m. MARTHA SHAW
1781–1825   1784–1824

EDWARD m.
MARY SULSTON

JOHN
1806–24

FRANCIS
1809–24

ELIZABETH
1811–1839

LEONARD
1812–?

MARTHA
1814–16

MARTHA m. THOMAS TIMMS
1816–86   1844   1819–?1880

CLEMENTINA m. JOHN WAINE
1821–88   1841   1820–1896

EDWIN
1818–24

3 sons
5 daughters

SEE TIMMS TREE

7 sons
1 daughter

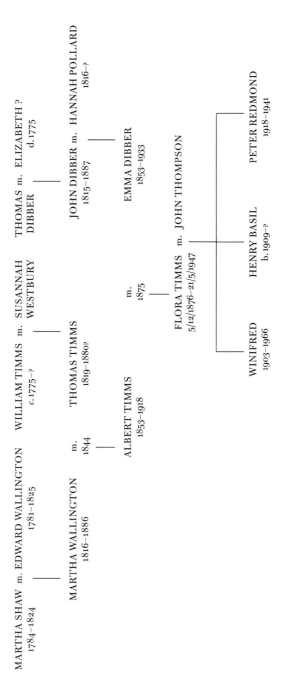

3. The Wallington and Timms family connections

13

4. The carrier formed a vital link between villages and their market towns. Flora herself travelled to Banbury on the carrier's cart from Juniper Hill. Here William Humphries, the Greatworth carrier who travelled to Banbury and Brackley is seen outside Mr Chester's bakery in Piddington, *c.*1900 (John Watts)

carried out, and the farm had been left in the possession of her husband Edward. On his death the surviving children continued living there but *'there being no fund whatever out of which provision can be made for their advancement in the world'* it was hoped the Court would give permission for the farm to be sold to pay off debts and give the children each their shares.

To complicate matters, other lands which were not mortgaged to Elizabeth Shaw had been settled on Martha Shaw and Edward Wallington at their marriage, which increased the size of the farm, and it would be detrimental to both to sell one without the other, but Edward's brother John refused to sell them unless told to do so by the court. The children also needed a Guardian to care for their interests.

After long and convoluted arguments the judge decided that Edward Wallington (the son of Martha and Edward) must pay off the principal and interest on the loan given by Elizabeth Shaw to free the farm from the provisions of her will, or else it must be sold, together with the disputed properties settled on Martha and Edward Wallington at their marriage, and the money could then be used to pay off the debt to Elizabeth if possible, otherwise to pay the bills of the tradesmen and then be divided equally between the surviving children. The case came back to Chancery on 4 August 1830 when the Master of the Court had sold the farm to the highest bidder, the Rev. John Cleobury of Piddington, who paid £900 for it. Thomas Stevens, a yeoman of Piddington, was made formal guardian of the children, as he had been acting for them since they were orphaned.

The Master reported that the money Martha Shaw had lent Edward and Martha Wallington had never been repaid nor had interest been paid on it so that the grand total owed to her estate £2859 19s 10½d. The costs amounted to £189 9s 9d. A suitable occupational rent for the property would be £42 a year from November 1816 to July 1830, totalling £576 16s.

Although the children had been receiving shares in the produce of the farm amounting to £73 16s a year and rents on four small cottages of £8 12s they were otherwise destitute and owed money to a number of local tradespeople for provisions, meat, malt and beer, flour, clothing, linen and hosiery, shoes, mercery and drapery, coals, carpenter's work, barley and a cow. Money was owed to Hannah Smith schoolmistress and Abraham Chapman schoolmaster, both of Islip, for board and education for the children. (For details see Appendix One).

Leonard wanted to be apprenticed to Frederick Indermance of Union Street, Southwark, London, as a cabinet maker and needed £70 to cover the cost of the apprenticeship, meat, drink and lodging until he came of age. Thomas Stevens was given money to pay off all the debts and told that any money left over was to be invested in 3% Consolidated Birminghams and the income used for the future maintenance of the children in case the money allocated from the case should prove insufficient. There cannot have been much left over as the sale of the farm brought in so much less than the money owed.

It was decided that the cost of completing the children's education should be taken from their shares, so after all the debts had been paid off the children received the following shares:

Piddington.

5. Piddington village scene, *c*.1900. (John Watts)

Elizabeth Wallington: £143 9s 11¾d less £37 15s 9¾d for education, total £105 14s 2d.

Martha Wallington: £143 9s 11¾d less £64 5s 5¾d for education, total £79 4s 6¾d

Clements Wallington: £143 9s 11 3/4d less £48 8s 3¾d for education, total £95 1s 8¾d

Leonard Wallington had to pay his debts and apprenticeship out of his share and was left with only £7 16s 6d.

Edward Wallington received £109 2s after his debts had been paid. He went on to marry his Mary Sulston and they had eight children.

This Chancery case seems to have been the origin of the family legend that Martha had inherited £1000—in fact she eventually received less than one tenth of that amount. It is possible that she inherited money from elsewhere, but this does not seem likely in view of the penurious situation revealed in the Chancery case and lack of relatives offering to help the children. It is not known where Martha lived after the sale of the farm, but she married Thomas Timms at Ambrosden by special licence on 18 November 1844, aged 28. Presumably as she had achieved her majority she would not have had to make the runaway match of family legend, even though her husband Thomas Timms was younger than she was, being 25 and, as he worked as a mason, might have been considered below her in status.

Thomas' father William Timms had been born in Bicester around 1775 and served in the Oxfordshire Militia in 1814. He married Susannah Westbury in 1802, and they had five children, of whom Thomas, born on 25 September 1819, was the youngest.

Flora wrote some interesting comments about the surname Timms to Leslie Castle in 1943:

> "Timms, of course, is a very old Thames Valley name. Most of the Timmses appear to have been either masons or boatbuilders, it was a regular craftsmens' name and I think must originally have been Thames, as I have seen it spelt "Tems" and "Teems" in old history books. A member of Parliament of the name of Tems was the only member to have courage to vote against the divorce of Catherine of Aragon, the ill-used queen of Henry VIII. I like to imagine him an ancestor."

It is not known definitely whether or not Thomas and Martha did own the hotel and livery stables in Oxford, which Flora called The Horse and

Rider, but considering their finances it seems unlikely. Certainly they were living in St Albans when their first child Anne Elizabeth was born in 1846 two years after their marriage, so if they did have premises in Oxford they did not stay not there long. By 1851 Thomas Timms was working as a mason and the family were living in North End, Buckingham, where Anne was baptised with her younger sister Jane in that year. Flora's father Albert was baptised in Buckingham on 23 July 1853 and the youngest son, Edwin was born on 19 July 1855.

Martha seems to have worked to supplement the family income, being described as a dressmaker of Gawcott Road, Buckingham, in the census returns of 1861 and 1871, although the ages given there are totally wrong: in 1861 Thomas' age is given as 46 when he was 42 and Martha's as 35, although she was 46, and in 1871 Thomas is said to be 49 instead of 52 and Martha has lost years to become 28 instead of 56! The 1871 census records that not only Thomas but his sons Albert and Edwin, aged 16 and 14 respectively, were working as masons and living at the same address. Although little is known about what happened to her uncle Edwin, Flora suggested in Lark Rise that he joined the Royal Engineers and served in Nova Scotia.

Flora remembered meeting her Aunt Jane, as a small child. She had apparently married a master builder who lived in Yorkshire, and seldom visited the family. Her display of wealth seems to have made Emma Timms, her sister-in-law, rather uncomfortable:

> "Jane was too dressy and 'set up' for her taste, she said. That morning, her luggage being still at the railway station, she was wearing the clothes she had travelled in, a long pleated dove–coloured gown with an apron arrangement drawn round and up and puffed over a bustle at the back, and, on her head, a tiny toque made entirely of purple velvet pansies . . ."

Lark Rise to Candleford, p. 37

Flora later wrote that at the outbreak of the Boer War, her brother Edwin was staying with relatives in Yorkshire, and immediately joined the West Yorkshire Regiment. It is likely that these relatives would have been Aunt Jane and her husband. Unfortunately Jane did not marry in Buckingham, and her husband's identity has not so far been traced.

After she was widowed, Martha went to live in Twyford, Buckinghamshire, with her daughter Ann, who had married shoemaker Thomas

Whiting—the Uncle Tom of Candleford, of whom more later. Martha was buried in Twyford on 10 August 1886, aged 69.

Although Flora could not truly claim kinship with the more aristocratic branch of the Wallington family, she would have been delighted to learn that through the Wallingtons and their Delafield ancestry she could claim kinship with Thomas and Matthew Arnold and the aristocracy. A cousin, Martha Delafield (1750–89) married William Arnold, a collector of customs from the Isle of Wight. Their son Thomas (1795–1842) was the headmaster of Rugby School immortalised in Tom Brown's Schooldays, and his son Matthew became a famous poet, so Flora can legitimately claim to have literary figures in her ancestry. Martha and William's daughter Lydia married Richard Ford William Lambart, 7th Earl of Cavan.

2

Ardley and Fewcott: The Dibber Family

꽃

Flora Thompson's mother, Emma Dibber, born in 1853, was brought up in Ardley, now known as Ardley with Fewcott, a small village north–west of Bicester. She later worked as nursemaid for the curate at Fewcott, then a separate village, part of the parish of Stoke Lyne. Emma's father John Dibber was recorded as living in Ardley in the 1851 census, having been baptised in Stoke Lyne on 26 September 1813. Their surname confusingly appears in several different forms in different documents—in the parish registers as Dibber, on Emma's marriage certificate as Dipper and on Flora's birth certificate as Lapper.

John Dibber, Flora's beloved grandfather, was the eldest son of Thomas Dibber, an agricultural labourer, and his first wife Elizabeth who went on to have six other children, two of whom, James and Harriet, died in infancy, and another, Ellen, who died aged 19. John's mother died aged 42, shortly after her youngest daughter Harriet was born and five years later his father Thomas was married again, to Hannah Andrews of Ardley and they had two more children. Hannah was recorded in the 1861 census as being a lace-maker.

John Dibber married another Hannah in 1835 when he was 21 and his bride 19. Hannah Pollard came from Hornton, north of Banbury, where her father John was a labourer, but it is not known whether, as Flora suggested, he was also a gamekeeper. Hannah was evidently considered a local beauty, nicknamed 'the Belle of Hornton', with luxuriant waist length blonde hair.

THE DIPPER OR DIBBER FAMILY

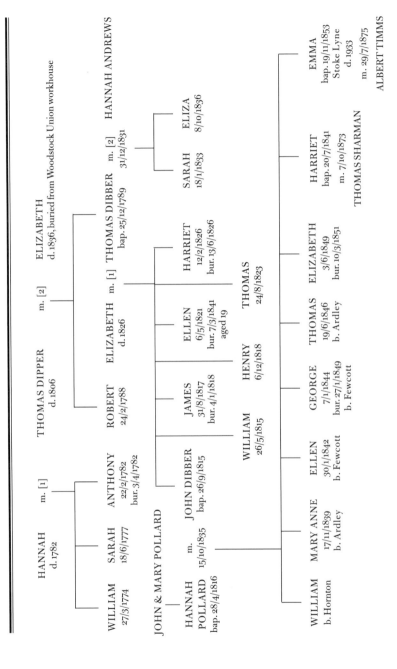

1. The family tree of the Dibber family

She always considered that one of her chief claims to fame was that she had once attracted the notice of a 'real lord', the son of her father's employer, who had seen her at his coming of age celebrations and singled her out to dance with him, preferring her to the more aristocratic young ladies there. He had told her that she was the prettiest girl in the county—a compliment she treasured for the rest of her life, but in those days there was no chance of any lasting romance between people of such differing classes. Flora wrote:

'It was difficult for Laura to connect the long, yellow hair and the white frock with blue ribbons worn at the coming-of-age fete with her grand-mother, for she saw her only as a thin, frail old woman who wore her grey hair parted like curtains and looped at the ears with little combs. Still, there was something which made her worth looking at. Laura's mother said it was because her features were good. "My mother", she would say, "will look handsome in her coffin. Colour goes and the hair turns grey, but the framework lasts."'

Lark Rise to Candleford, p.94

Hannah was a rather self-centred woman who expected to be cherished. She loved good clothes and wanted pretty things around her, decorating her bedroom with pictures and ornaments and making it comfortable with feather cushions and a silk-patchwork quilt. She spent hours reading romantic novelettes which she exchanged with her friends. When she visited the Timms family in Juniper she was always allocated the best chair by the fire and Emma gave her the best tea she could provide.

John and Hannah's eldest son was born in Hornton, but the family moved to Ardley, where Mary Ann was born in 1839. They can be found in the census returns for Ardley in 1861 and 1871, retiring to Cottisford before 1881. They had six surviving children. William, their eldest, aged 23, was living with his mother-in-law Hannah Gibbard in Ardley in 1861. Emma, their youngest, was born in 1853. Hannah outlived her husband, and after his death in 1887 she left Juniper to live with her son William, and their abandoned house disintegrated. Hannah was too full of her own concerns to appreciate the sacrifices her husband made for her.

Flora obviously adored her grandfather, John Dibber, remembering him as a man in his seventies with white hair and beard setting off his bright blue eyes, although he could be strict and demanded high standards of behaviour from her. Although he was described merely as an agricultural labourer in the census returns, Flora wrote that he worked as an eggler, travelling round the area in a horse and trap to buy eggs from cottagers and farmers which he resold to shops and at markets.

John Dibber was a religious man, attending every service in the church and often going to the church at other times to pray. He had later become a local preacher, walking to other villages to preach in cottage meeting houses, and had a reputation for inspired preaching. As an old man he attended Church of England services again, enjoying the music he could no longer play: he had played the violin with the village musicians in Ardley church and the choir and musicians came to practise in their cottage in the evenings. His skills as a violinist were also in demand for weddings and feasts and at other local gatherings in neighbours' houses. When Flora asked what had happened to his violin she was told by her mother that he had sold it to raise money when her grandmother had been ill. She seems to have been the only one to realise what a sacrifice it must have been for him. He also had to give up smoking when he retired, because they had little to live on, even though a coal–merchant brother sent them a small allowance. What he hated most was that he no longer had money for presents for his family. By this time he and his wife had moved to a little round house in Cottisford near the Timms family so he managed to visit the end house each day, bringing with him something in season from the garden, such as a marrow, peas or raspberries.

He was badly afflicted with rheumatism in old age, which constricted his movements, so that as his health declined he could no longer walk to church, then even the journey to Flora's house became too much for him. Eventually he was confined to his bed in the attic bedroom he had considerately chosen to sleep in so that Hannah would not be disturbed by his tossing and turning, or woken up when he rose early to read the Bible:

> "Gradually his limbs became so locked he could not turn over in bed without help. Giving to and doing for others was over for him. He would lie upon his back for hours, his tired old blue eyes fixed upon the picture nailed on the wall at the foot of his bed. It was the only coloured thing in the room; the rest was bare whiteness. It was of the Crucifixion, and, printed above the crown of thorns were the words:
>   This have I done for thee.
> And underneath the pierced and bleeding feet:
>   What hast thou done for me?
> His two years' uncomplaining endurance of excruciating pain answered for him."

Lark Rise to Candleford, pp. 93–4

2. The village band playing for the feast of the Stoke Lyne Friendly Society outside the Peyton Arms. Flora's grandfather, John Dibber, played at similar feasts and gatherings. Front row, left to right: Harry White in a straw hat, Joseph Beasley with stick and straw hat, Rodney Denny (son of the licensee George Denny) with a banjo, and to his right, Fred Butler. Back Row: third from left with beard and a bowler hat is John Coggins, next to him is Lewis Hickman, bailiff at Swift's House. To his right is Sir Algernon Peyton of Swift's house, Stoke Lyne, and at the base of the flagpole stands Elisha Allen, stone carter from Fritwell. On the end is Harry Beasley. Others known to have been present on the photograph are: Vincent and Ben Golder, Tom White, Alfred Richardson (father of Alf Richardson, the Bicester postman) and Charles Brandrick. (John Watts, characters identified by Harold French and Gordon Allen)

John Dibber was buried in Cottisford church on 30 March 1887.

When they were younger, John and Hannah had lived in Ardley, which had never been a large village, although it had a small twelfth century castle built by the Norman Hugh of Avranches. The village was in decline when John Dibber knew it, with a population in 1821 of 191. For much of the century it boasted a wonderful rector in John Lowe, who was mentioned by Flora in *Lark Rise to Candleford*. Her mother Emma must have told her enough about him to leave a vivid impression. He became rector in 1815 as a young man of about 24 and remained the incumbent until 1873 when he was in his 80s. He fell in love at first sight with Susannah, the daughter of his predecessor Thomas Hind, and they married after a short engagement. He also had parishes in Yorkshire, so did not become resident in Ardley until 1833, using curates to run the parish until then. After his wife's death her sister Ann Hind lived for a while at the Rectory and became a great benefactor to the parish. He became much loved in the parish and revived interest in the church, and in one year preached about 95 sermons. He

3. The 17th century rectory, now known as Ardley House, where John Lowe, rector of Ardley from 1815–73, lived. Emma Dibber, Flora's mother, often visited here as a child for singing and writing lessons. (Ardley Local History Society)

attracted congregations of between 50 and 60 in the mornings and 70 to 80 at evening services. He commented on his parishioners that his only problems were "unbelief and hardness of heart. These are my great hindrances, and, in a few cases, the love of drinking." (From Wilberforce's Visitations, quoted in the *Victoria History of the County of Oxfordshire* Vol. VI, 1959 p.13). He offered to take on the oversight of the residents of nearby Fewcott in 1840, as many of them preferred to attend Ardley church rather than make the longer journey to their parish church at Stoke Lyne, but the patron Dr Marcham refused his offer.

The Old Rectory where he lived was a seventeenth century house, taxed on four hearths in 1665, much enlarged and altered over the centuries, with major alterations in 1860 and again in 1874. It is now called Ardley House. In 1871 John Lowe, then aged 80, was living there with his niece Mary Ann Willoughby, aged 42, Eliza Wilkins, a lady's maid, aged 47, Lydia, a 50 year old cook, Sarah Gulliver the housemaid aged 28 and 25 year old George Surridge, who acted as footman and domestic servant.

John Lowe and the Vicar of Stoke Lyne together supported a small day school in the village by 1854, for which the 30 pupils paid one penny a week. Emma Dibber would have attended this as a child. In 1861 a larger school for 60 children was built by the Duke of Marlborough, subsequently enlarged with money from Miss Anne Hind, which became affiliated to the National Society in 1862. The school closed in 1914 and the actual building was physically moved to Sandford St Martin in the 1920s.

The Dibbers lived in a cottage near the church, so the school would have been opposite. Flora wrote that Emma had caught the eye of the rector's sister, who had taken her under her wing:

"Yet she had brains of her own and her education had been above the average for her station in life ... At the time when she was a small girl ... the incumbent of the parish had been an old man and with him had lived his still more aged sister. This lady, whose name was Miss Lowe, had become very fond of the pretty, fair-haired little girl at the churchyard cottage and had had her at the Rectory every day out of school hours. Little Emma had a sweet voice and she was supposed to go there for singing lessons; but she had learned other things, too, including old world manners and to write a beautiful antique hand with delicate open-looped pointed letters and long 's's', such as her instructress and other young ladies had been taught in the last quarter of the 18th century.

4. Group outside Ardley School, which Emma Dibber attended. (Ardley Local History Society)

Miss Lowe was then nearly eighty, and had long been dead when Laura, at two and a half years old, had been taken by her mother to see the by then very aged Rector. The visit was one of her earliest memories, which survived as an indistinct impression of twilight in a room with dark green walls and the branch of a tree against the outside of the window; and, more distinctly, a pair of trembling, veiny hands putting something smooth and cold and round into her own . . . The old gentleman, it appeared, had given her a china mug which had been his sister's in her nursery days. It had stood on the mantelpiece at the end house for years, a beautiful old piece with a design of heavy green foliage on a ground of translucent whiteness. Afterwards it got broken, which was strange in that careful house; but Laura carried the design in her mind's eye for the rest of her life and would sometimes wonder if it accounted for her lifelong love of green and white in conjunction."

Lark Rise to Candleford, p. 39

It is likely that 'Miss Lowe' was in fact Anne Hind, John Lowe's sister-in-law rather than sister, who was younger than Flora suggested, being 66 in 1861. Her encouragement does seem to have given Emma Dibber a much better education than an agricultural labourer's daughter would otherwise have obtained, so she may in turn have passed this on to her daughter Flora, indirectly helping her to achieve her potential. The story of Flora's visit to the Rectory and the gift of the cup is apocryphal as John Lowe died in March 1874, two years before she was born.

When Emma was old enough to leave school she became a nursemaid, and went to work in the rectory (now renamed Weavers and situated next to the nineteenth century schoolhouse) in Fewcott, just down the road. Enclosure had taken place in the village in 1794, which increased the value of the land, but the population dropped from 220 in 1841 to 160 twenty years later, and continued to decline.

5. Ardley church, attended by Flora's grandparents, the Dibbers, and her mother, and where John Dibber played the violin in the choir. (Ardley Local History Society)

The Fewcott parishioners were expected to go to Stoke Lyne church but some residents preferred to go to Ardley which was much nearer, so Miss Anne Hind, sister–in–law of the Rector of Ardley, left £2000 in her will when she died in 1870 to provide a curacy for Fewcott and a further £1000 for the vicarage of Stoke Lyne. She had written to the Rural Dean in 1865 expressing her intentions:

> "I, Anne Hind, having purchased nearly four acres of land with a cottage, a barn, and some small out–buildings in the hamlet of Fewcote, near Ardley, amounting in value to £630 (and when the necessary alterations now begun in the cottage, etc., are completed, the value may be safely stated at £700) do declare that it is my desire and intention to bequeath the land and cottage, etc., etc., to Queen Anne's Bounty in trust for the benefit of the Church of England, and of the parishes of Ardley and Stoke Lyne to which the hamlet of Fewcote is now annexed. If the hamlet of Fewcote should be hereafter annexed to the Parish of Ardley, it would then be my desire that the 4 acres of land with the cottage and outbuildings which I have purchased in Fewcote should become an augmentation of the living of Ardley for the benefit of that living, and of the poor parishioners of Fewcote; if on the contrary, the hamlet of Fewcote should remain as it is, a part of the parish of Stoke Lyne, then it would be my desire that the said portion of land at Fewcote and the cottage aforesaid and the adjoining buildings should be annexed to the living of Stoke Lyne in order to secure the residence of a Curate in the hamlet of Fewcote . . . "

Quoted in J.C.Blomfield, *History of the Present Deanery of Bicester*, Part VIII, 1894

Miss Hind had a schoolroom built in 1865 and assigned the cottage as a residence for the Curate of Ardley, Rev. H. J. Joscelyne, on condition he held services on Sunday evenings in the school room. He was the first curate to use the new church which was built in Fewcott, consecrated to All Saints in 1871, which operated as a chapel of Stoke Lyne. It cost £900 to build and was designed by H. Woodyer, comprising a simple nave with apsidal chancel and an open bell turret.

Emma obviously enjoyed working for Rev. Joscelyne and his family, and seems to have been treated more as a member of the family than as a servant. The 1871 census shows the residents of Fewcott Parsonage as being the curate, Henry Joscelyne, aged 44, his wife Mary Louise, aged 36, their children Louise Elizabeth, aged 14, Henry Maurice, aged 11, Herbert Cathcart,

6. The former rectory at Fewcott nest to the old village school where Emma Dibber lived when she was employed as nursemaid by the curate Rev. Henry Joscelyne. The house is now known as 'Weavers'.

aged 7, Alice Emma, aged 6, Arthur Edwin aged 4, Ethel aged 2 and Edward Walter, aged 3 months, together with their servants, Emma Dipper aged seventeen and Susan Hayward aged 16. Flora described how her mother used to tell her about life on Fewcott Rectory, disguising the name of the family to Johnstone:

> " The living was small and the Rectory was poor, but three maids had been possible in those days, a cook-general, a young housemaid, and Nurse Emma. They must have been needed in that large, rambling old house, in which lived the Rector and his wife, their nine children, three maids, and often three or four young men pupils. They all had such jolly, happy times she said, all of them, family and maids and pupils, singing glees and part songs in the drawing-room in the evening."
>
> *Lark Rise to Candleford*, pp.39–40

31

Emma held up the parsonage children as paragons of virtue to her own children, but in that perhaps she was exaggerating, as Flora recalled that when she was taken to visit them the boys pulled her hair and one of them dressed up as a priest, using the cook's apron as a surplice, and proceeded to bury Flora's doll in the orchard!

Emma was a bright, attractive girl, much appreciated by the family, and also influenced by them:

> "She was a slight, graceful girl with a wild-rose complexion and hair the colour of a new penny which she parted in the middle and drew down to a knot at the back of her head because a gentleman of the family, where she had been nurse to the children before her marriage, had told her she ought always to do it like that.
>
> 'A pocket Venus,' she said he had called her. 'But quite nicely,' she hastened to assure her listener, 'for he was a married gentleman with no nonsense about him.'
>
> *Lark Rise to Candleford*, p. 272

When Mr. Joscelyne moved to Fingest-cum-Ibstone in Buckinghamshire in 1879, his parishioners presented him with farewell gifts of a tea and coffee service and a purse of sovereigns. Emma remained friendly with the eldest daughter Louise, renamed Lily in Lark Rise, who must have been 22 rather than 17 when Emma took her family to visit the Rectory in 1879 before they left the parish. Flora recalled that as she accompanied them for some of the walk home she chatted to Emma about her admirers. She must have retained a great affection for Emma and her family as she sent regular parcels of books and toys at Christmas and carried on corresponding with Emma into the 1920s.

The 1871 census records only seven children rather than the nine Flora mentions, so perhaps older boys were away at school, or more were born after 1871 and perhaps an additional servant was employed after this date. Emma probably remained with the family until her marriage in July 1875 when she moved to Juniper Hill.

3

Juniper Hill: *Lark Rise*

୫ୈ

"The hamlet stood on a gentle rise in the flat, wheat-growing north-east corner of Oxfordshire. We will call it Lark Rise because of the great number of skylarks which made the surrounding fields their springboards and nested on the bare earth between the rows of green corn . . . Old men could remember when the Rise, covered with juniper bushes, stood in the midst of a furzy heath—common land, which had come under the plough after the passing of the Enclosure Acts. Some of the ancients still occupied cottages on land which had been ceded to their fathers as 'squatters' rights', and probably all the small plots upon which the houses stood had originally been so ceded. In the eighteen-eighties the hamlet consisted of about thirty cottages and an inn, not built in rows, but dotted down anywhere within a more or less circular group. A deeply rutted cart track surrounded the whole, and separate houses or groups of houses were connected by a network of pathways. Going from one part of the hamlet to another was called 'going round the Rise', and the plural of 'house' was not 'houses', but 'housen'. The only shop was a small general one kept in the back kitchen of the inn. The church and school were in the mother village, a mile and a half away.

A road flattened the circle at one point. It had been cut when the heath was enclosed for convenience in fieldwork and to connect the main Oxford road with the mother village and a series of other villages beyond. From the hamlet it led on the one hand to church and school, and on the other to the main road, or the turnpike, as it was still called, and so to the market town where the Saturday shopping was done."

Lark Rise to Candleford, pp. 17–18

1. 1882 Ordnance Survey map of the village showing the main road through the village which leads to the turnpike, and the curved road which Flora called 'The Rise'. The Timms' cottage was situated close to the number '17' marked on the map, set away from the path, with Queenie's cottage in front of it. Flora renamed the 'Fox' public house 'The Wagon and Horses'. (Centre for Oxfordshire Studies)

Flora's evocative description of her village is one of the most memorable passages of *Lark Rise* and is still apt today, although several of the houses Flora knew have been demolished or disintegrated and been replaced by new ones. Thanks to the fame of *Lark Rise to Candleford* the little village of Juniper Hill, which Flora rechristened Lark Rise is now part of a conservation area. Yet anyone visiting in 1753 would have seen nothing there except bleak empty heathland.

The first houses were built on the Juniper Hill site in 1754, paid for by a poor rate, as recorded in the Cottisford parish records:

"MEMORANDUM: Two Cottages Erected in the Year of our Lord 1754 on Juniper Hill in the Parish of Cotsford in the County of Oxon for the use of the poor of the sd parish. Expenses of which Houses or Cottages amounted to the sum of £28 7s 6d.

Built by a rate charged on the landholders, viz. Richd Eyre Esq., the Rev. Jas Smith, Rector, Mr John Westcar, Henry Sansom, John Tebby, Thos. Jarvis, Robt. Day, landholders.

Recorded in J.C. Blomfield, *History of the Present Deanery of Bicester* Part III, 1887

Blomfield explained why it acquired the name of Juniper Hill:

"On some ground to the N.E. of the village, the low evergreen bushy shrub, known as the Common Juniper, grew in abundance. Its hard wood was useful fuel, and its spicy berries may have been beneficial as medicines. Hence this spot came to be known in recent times as Juniper Hill."

op. cit. p.37

It seems extraordinary to our eyes to build two houses in the middle of nowhere, but Cottisford, the mother village, which Flora calls Fordlow, came under the tight control of Eton College, so the type of resident could be severely restricted, and the College evidently did not want to have the poor people living too close. Two more cottages were built soon afterwards, then only few more until the nineteenth century. Some of those built then were the work of squatters, building a hearth and a chimney and lighting a fire in it between dawn and dusk, which gave them a claim to the piece of land, although it had a dubious legal basis. Such people would have a measure of independence as they 'owned' their own houses. Some cottages may have been built specifically for letting to agricultural labourers—at enclosure several cottages were owned by the Fermor trustees of Tusmore Park. When the enclosure of Cottisford Heath was first authorised in 1848 Juniper labourers became notorious because of their violent opposition to it over several years, tearing down the notices about enclosure and attacking surveyors. They were rightly concerned that enclosure would deprive them of their right to graze animals on waste ground, cut wood for fires and sedge for the livestock, which supplemented their wages as agricultural labourers.

The local magistrate, J.B.Parry of Cottisford House, wrote a letter in 1853 which indicated that he had little sympathy with these independent-minded, possibly lawless, labourers:

"My object in reference to the Juniper cottagers is to have them put ... on the usual terms on which cottages are let, viz liable to eviction after a week's notice, with a view to secure their good behaviour, or to get rid of any who shall be guilty of poaching, or other misconduct, and my idea is that the best way to bring about that state of things would be to propose allowing them to remain in their cottages as weekly tenants at some small rent, say 6d a week, with a good-size plot of garden ground included, and to let it be understood that they should not be disturbed during their lives if no complaints were made of them, or they did not become chargeable to the parish ...Those who could not accept such terms should, of course, be evicted at once ... It is quite essential to the welfare of this and the adjoining manors that none of these fellows should be left in the position of freeholders."

The disruptions continued until 1853 when the Bicester petty sessions finally issued warrants of ejectment against 42 Juniper men who had no true legal claim to their land, including several members of the Moss family, (some of the Moss family changed their surname in embarrassment at the connection with these rough goings-on) and some agreed to settle, so escaped ejection. Four men who could prove their ownership of their land were allocated small plots in the enclosure award. The case was reported in the *Oxford Chronicle* of 30 June 1853, which stated that the labourers who had "resided at Juniper Hill for various periods, and then formed a colony" were charged with not giving up their land, and warrants were issued for their ejectment. They had put up such strong resistance that it was feared that the men would not leave gracefully but the fears proved unfounded:

"The Juniper Hill Ejectments—It will be remembered that a few weeks since the authorities under the Cottisford Enclosure act obtained, at the Bicester petty sessions, warrants of ejectment against about 40 working people who were holding cottages on land at Juniper Hill, in that parish, and who had there formed a colony, and who looked upon interference with their "territorial" possessions as a measure to be resisted. From threats that had been made it was thought that on the ejectments being enforced the occupants would lawfully resist and that it would be necessary to have the assistance of those skilled in the arts of war. This, however, has not been necessary, and an arrangement has been come to. On Tuesday and Wednesday last the authorities, to the number of about 20, proceeded to take possession of the occupancies of those who had not previously made terms with them. The constables' men had pick axes, etc., for demolishing the buildings in case such extreme measures should appear necessary. They, however, were not. All the defendants gave up possession. In return they are to have the crops from the land, and to have 14 years leases at 5s. per year, of their residence and garden ground.

Oxford Chronicle, 20 August 1853

John Collett, a parish constable, did not at all approve of the way the squatters were being treated and was found guilty of misconduct because he dared to express his support for them, and fined £2 8s together with 12 shillings costs.

Flora later wrote about Old Sally and her husband Dick, who were based on Sarah and Richard Moss, who married in 1869. Both Sarah's first husband George Fox and her second Richard Moss were involved in the riots and Richard was a notorious poacher who had been specifically threatened with eviction. Surprisingly Flora does not mention the disturbances at enclosure at all in her writing, although they took place only twenty odd years before she was born.

By 1871 there were 33 cottages in Juniper, five of which were unoccupied. The census returns of 1871, 1881 and 1891 tell us about the village as Flora would have known it and give clues as to the identity of some of Flora's characters, although she has changed many of the details. In 1871 there were 37 labourers, the youngest of whom was twelve, two shepherds, a shoe maker (Thomas Whiting, who became Flora's Uncle Tom, of whom more later), one labourer and grocer, one publican and grocer, one man with no occupation, one laundress, one dress maker and 28 scholars (schoolchildren), the oldest of whom was eleven. There was some continuity of occupation as nine of the names recorded were of the same families as in the 1801 census: Collett, Fox, Hall, Judas, Moss, Price, Sabbin (presumably the same as Savin in 1801), Tuffrey and White.

In 1881 the number of labourers had increased to 39, still two shepherds, a gardener, one publican, one tailor, and Albert Timms as stone mason, one laundress and 29 scholars. In 1891 there were still 39 labourers, three shepherds, one stone mason and mason (Albert Timms), one publican, two engine drivers, one carpenter, one thatcher, and female occupations included one servant (at the pub), a seamstress and a sick nurse, with only 23 scholars.

The Timms Family

Albert Timms, called 'Robert' in Lark Rise to Candleford, is said to have come to the area when he was working on the repairs to some local churches, so perhaps he rented a property in Juniper. He soon seems to have found friends there, if he did not know them before, as he and his wife Emma Dibber were both witnesses to the marriage of Emma's elder sister Harriet to Thomas Sharman at Cottisford church in 1873 (Thomas died young, at the age of 32, in 1880, and Harriet left Juniper). Perhaps surprisingly Albert and Emma themselves married in Cottisford on 29 July 1875, rather than in Ardley where her parents lived. The witnesses at their wedding were Albert's sister Ann and Thomas Whiting, who lived in Juniper at that time and married Ann on 17 April 1876, with Albert and Emma as witnesses. Albert and Emma rented a cottage in Juniper Hill, near to Watford Tunnel Cottage where her sister Harriet was living. Albert got a job as stonemason with a firm in Brackley, whose premises were situated on the road to Banbury, where he worked for the same firm for 35 years. He had to walk three miles there and three miles back, and sometimes many more miles to the site where he was working. His hours were from six in the morning until five in the afternoon.

Albert was initially proud of his ability as a stonemason, although he had not undertaken a formal apprenticeship. As a young man he built a little workshop on the side of the cottage, and Flora remembered seeing some of his carvings used as ornaments around the house—a lion, a baby's head and lilies of the valley growing at the base of a tree trunk. There was a wide variety of work in the area at that time, as country houses were being built and extended, and he may have worked on Tusmore House which was being extended at this time. As well as the elaborate work required for large houses he could turn his hand to carving a tombstone, or repairing a cottage or building a wall, or even bricklaying.

Albert married at the age of 21, and Flora was born eighteen months later so it is not surprising that Flora remembers him as a handsome young man:

> "As Laura first remembered him he was a slim, upright young man in the late twenties, with dark, fiery eyes and raven-black hair, but fair, fresh-coloured complexion. On account of the dusty-white nature of his work, he usually wore clothes of some strong light-grey worsted material. Years after he had died, an old and embittered man, she could see him, a white apron rolled up around his middle, a basket of tools slung over his shoulder and a black billycock hat set at an angle on his head, swinging along the crown of the road on his way home from work."
>
> *Lark Rise to Candleford*, p. 262

As a craftsman he earned slightly more than the ten shillings a week of the agricultural labourer so when the family moved to the End House, where Flora grew up, they were able to afford two shillings and sixpence a week to rent the double cottage. Albert was more intelligent than most of his neighbours and enjoyed himself at election time, standing on a plank supported by beer barrels to explain Gladstone's policies in an amusing way. For many years he and Emma kept talking about moving away from Juniper to find better schooling for the children, perhaps to a town, but something always seemed to happen to put it off. Albert became frustrated in his work, and his use of his skills seems to have declined as he grew older, as in 1891 he was described as a stone and brick mason. He preferred the more complex work he had done in churches to general building, but he was never able to better himself, grew depressed and turned to drink, so that the income he brought home was irregular, which must have caused the careful Emma many problems. However his sisters had married well, so parcels of cast off clothes helped Emma to dress her family better than most.

Flora used the character of a stonemason in several pieces of her writing, though the details differ in each instance and we cannot be sure how much she drew on the character of her father in writing them. In an unpublished fragment of a book entitled *The Stithy*, she wrote about the death of a stone-

THE TIMMS

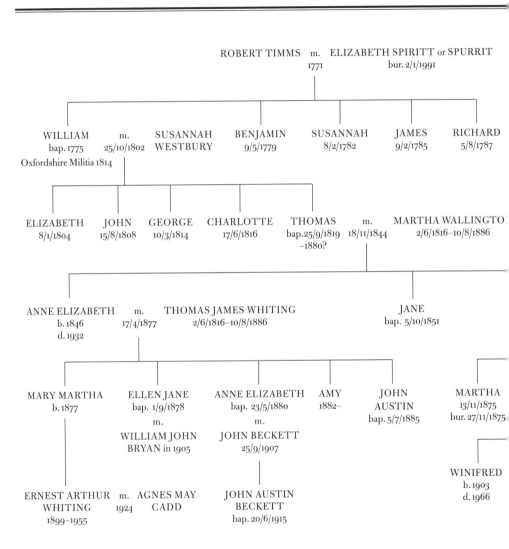

ROBERT TIMMS m. ELIZABETH SPIRITT or SPURRIT
1771 bur. 2/1/1991

WILLIAM m. SUSANNAH BENJAMIN SUSANNAH JAMES RICHARD
bap. 1775 25/10/1802 WESTBURY 9/5/1779 8/2/1782 9/2/1785 5/8/1787
Oxfordshire Militia 1814

ELIZABETH JOHN GEORGE CHARLOTTE THOMAS m. MARTHA WALLINGTO
8/1/1804 15/8/1808 10/3/1814 17/6/1816 bap.25/9/1819 18/11/1844 2/6/1816–10/8/1886
–1880?

ANNE ELIZABETH m. THOMAS JAMES WHITING JANE
b. 1846 17/4/1877 2/6/1816–10/8/1886 bap. 5/10/1851
d. 1932

MARY MARTHA ELLEN JANE ANNE ELIZABETH AMY JOHN MARTHA
b. 1877 bap. 1/9/1878 bap. 23/5/1880 1882– AUSTIN 13/11/1875
m. m. bap. 5/7/1885 bur. 27/11/1875
WILLIAM JOHN JOHN BECKETT
BRYAN in 1905 25/9/1907

WINIFRED
b. 1903
d. 1966

ERNEST ARTHUR m. AGNES MAY JOHN AUSTIN
WHITING 1924 CADD BECKETT
1899–1955 bap. 20/6/1915

2. Family tree of the Timms family.

FAMILY

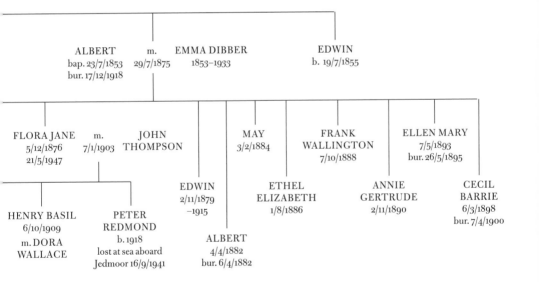

ALBERT   m.   EMMA DIBBER
bap. 23/7/1853   29/7/1875   1853–1933
bur. 17/12/1918

EDWIN
b. 19/7/1855

FLORA JANE   m.   JOHN
5/12/1876   7/1/1903   THOMPSON
21/5/1947

MAY
3/2/1884

FRANK
WALLINGTON
7/10/1888

ELLEN MARY
7/5/1893
bur. 26/5/1895

HENRY BASIL
6/10/1909
m. DORA
WALLACE

PETER
REDMOND
b. 1918
lost at sea aboard
Jedmoor 16/9/1941

EDWIN
2/11/1879
–1915

ETHEL
ELIZABETH
1/8/1886

ANNIE
GERTRUDE
2/11/1890

CECIL
BARRIE
6/3/1898
bur. 7/4/1900

ALBERT
4/4/1882
bur. 6/4/1882

mason, who left a widow and two children. It was written in the first person, and seems to contain some elements of Albert's character:

> "My father had not been very good to us. He had been a drunkard with all the faults of his kind; weak-willed, unstable, mean and prodigal by turns; a poor broken-down creature, puffed up to the last by a fancied superiority to the labouring people amongst whom we lived. A fancy based upon a tradition of blue blood in his veins and a striking presence."
>
> (Harry Ransom Humanities Research Center, The University of Texas at Austin)

The same stonemason character was reused, with almost the same phrases in places, in another unpublished book, *Gates of Eden*, so Flora was evidently influenced by the world of the stonemason, and by the character of her father in particular.

In *Still Glides the Stream*, she featured Thomas Hearne, an elderly stonemason who took too much of a pride in his job and spent too long perfecting the work for the taste of the new owner of the firm he worked for, making his work too expensive.

Emma was a pretty girl of 22 when she married Albert Timms. She took care with her appearance and her clothes, and when Flora and Edmund were small delighted in taking them for walks round the local roads in their wickerwork pram, a rarity in the village. She had to develop the art of making do and mending to maintain the family's standard of living as the money she received from Albert became more erratic, but she always made sure that she kept her head high and maintained the family's reputation in the village. Having worked as a nursemaid she was good with her children: strict but fair in her discipline and kind. She told wonderful fairy stories, some extending over several nights, and it was perhaps part of this imagination which flourished in her daughter. She does appear to have favoured her boys above the girls, particularly Edmund, and Flora seems to have felt that she was less loved than he was, and in consequence was not that close to her mother as she grew older. They did share happy memories though, and confidences, particularly just before Flora went to work in Fringford, and it was to Flora that Emma would talk of her father, John Dibber, after his death.

Emma and Albert rented two cottages in Juniper before they settled on the End House, situated half way round the Rise:

"Looking at the hamlet from a distance, one house would have been seen, a little apart, and turning its back on its neighbours, as though about to run away into the fields. It was a small grey stone cottage with a thatched roof, a green-painted door and a plum tree trained up the wall to the eaves."

Lark Rise to Candleford, p.20

3. Emma Timms, nee Dibber, Flora's mother.
(Henry Westbury)

The cottage had two small bedrooms, and Albert used his skills to improve it, adding a second downstairs room which they called the wash-house, and put in an oven grate so that they could roast the Sunday joint. Emma made the cottage welcoming, priding herself on keeping the furniture immaculately polished—never a lick and a promise for her—and decorating it with bright crockery and red and black rugs, (probably rag rugs), warmed the tile floor.

The Timms family were lucky in having their own well, as not all the cottages had one, and their earth closet was situated well away from the house to keep unpleasant smells to a minimum. The living room door led straight into the garden and the children often played there, relishing especially playing in the jungle-like tangle of growth of currant and gooseberry bushes and raspberry canes. Flora says that they rented the cottage from Mrs Herring, who was married to a retired stud groom and had lived in the village for a while.

The End House would now be almost unrecognisable to Flora, because most of it has been pulled down and rebuilt, leaving only one wall the same, and the thatch has been replaced by slates. A small plaque on the wall reveals it to be Flora's house.

Flora was born on 5 December 1876, probably in Watford Tunnel Cottage (now demolished) in Juniper, where Emma's sister Harriet lived, 'for convenience'. Later Emma often sent the elder children away when she was expecting the next baby, and there was a general pretence to the children that there was no pregnancy until the baby actually arrived. Flora was

4. Watford Tunnel cottage (now demolished), the birthplace of Flora Thompson, from a drawing by Lynton Lamb. (Oxford University Press)

5. Flora in a typical pose with a book. (Henry Westbury)

the eldest surviving daughter. She grew into a quiet, dreamy child, shy and diffident compared with the bouncy village children. She never found it easy to make friends, and always felt a little different from the children around her. As she grew up she was expected to help with her younger siblings, and Emma fondly imagined that she too would become a nursemaid, but changed her mind about her suitability when she saw that Flora would much rather read a book than pay any attention to small children.

Flora's favourite brother Edwin ('Edmund' in *Lark Rise*) was baptised on 2 November 1879. They always remained close, even though separated physically in adulthood. Both were quiet children:

> "Edmund was at that time a quiet, thoughtful little boy, apt to ask questions which it puzzled his mother to answer. The neighbours said he thought too much and ought to be made to play more; but they liked him because of his good looks and quaint, old-fashioned good manners ...
>
> He was a small slender child with blue eyes and regular features. When she had dressed him for their afternoon walk, his mother would kiss him and exclaim: 'I do declare he might be anybody's child. I can't see any difference between him and a young lord, and as for intelligence, he's too intelligent.'"
>
> *Lark Rise to Candleford*, pp. 267–8

As he grew older Edwin certainly knew his own mind. His mother wanted him to be apprenticed to a carpenter, but he had ideas of working on the land, considered in those days a badly paid and dead-end job, being an engine driver, or becoming a soldier and travelling abroad. In the end he was able to do two of those things. He left school to become an agricultural labourer at the age of 11, perhaps surprisingly early as he was an intelligent boy, who would have benefited from the opportunity to stay on longer at school. Perhaps the growing family meant that Albert could not afford to keep him at school any longer.

His ambition to be a soldier was achieved at the outbreak of the Boer War. Edwin was staying in Yorkshire, probably with Aunt Jane, when war was declared, and the 19-year old immediately went off to enlist in the West Yorkshire Regiment. Flora, who was then working at Grayshott Post Office, saw him off one snowy Sunday at Aldershot station; she was full of apprehension for his safety, while he was glowing with enthusiasm about the great adventure he was about to undertake.

6. Edwin Timms, Flora's favourite brother, in uniform, probably taken when he went off to fight in the Boer War. (Henry Westbury)

7. Edwin Timms in uniform, taken while he was serving in India. He went back into the army, as a Private in the 3rd Company, Second Battalion, the Eastern Ontario Regiment, to fight in the 1st World War, and was killed in his first week in the trenches. His obituary reported that his last words to his mother were "*Don't fret, mother, when I go into battle my last thoughts are for you and my God.*" (Henry Westbury)

8. Frank Timms, Flora's bother, who emigrated to Australia to become a fruit farmer. (Henry Westbury)

9. Betty Timms, Flora's younger sister, also became a writer and had her children's book *The Little Grey Men of the Moor* published. (Henry Westbury)

Edwin was lucky to survive the Boer War as he was taken prisoner while scouting and abandoned alone in the veldt, one enemy soldier probably saving his life by flinging him a half-empty water bottle as he rode off. It took him three days walking, parched with thirst, before he reached a Boer homestead where, despite his being her enemy, an old woman filled his water bottle.

His regiment was sent straight to India after the war, where he served for five years. He then spent a couple of years working for poor wages as a farm labourer in England before deciding to emigrate to Canada. Flora, by then married, travelled up to Juniper for a fortnight to be with the family and see him before he left. As he was working long hours on a farm, her time with him was necessarily brief. They managed to have one long walk together, talking of their childhood, and of Edwin's travels, and he claimed that the sights which had most impressed him were York Minster and the Taj Mahal. This was the last time the two were to meet. Edwin loved Canada, and seemed set to stay there for life, but the First World War took him back into the army. He joined the Eastern Ontario Regiment and had a brief home leave before embarking for France. Flora was unable to travel up to Oxfordshire to see him as her children were ill and the weather was bad. Three weeks after his arrival in France he was killed in action.

Flora heard about his death second hand one sunny April morning. She had felt that things were beginning to look better for her, and the children had recovered, when one of her own letters to him was returned to her, marked in pencil "Killed in Action". She should have been informed earlier, but apparently the official letter was misdirected. Flora was devastated and grieved bitterly for the death of such a beloved brother, but later she was philosophical:

> "... she came to feel in later life that in the matter of his death Edmund was indeed happy, for he was a soldier by his own choice and he died a soldier's death on the battlefield. Unlike some who fall in warfare he had not to relinquish life before he had well tasted it, and unlike others, he left behind him no brood of young children to face the world fatherless. He went the way of the old heroes of his childhood, in the prime of his manhood, fighting for a cause he wholeheartedly believed in, and went swiftly and suddenly in the heat of battle, a happy warrior."
>
> *Heatherley*, pp. 288–9

Edwin was buried in Woods Cemetery in Zillebeke, Belgium, and is commemorated on the war memorial in Cottisford church. Flora never forgot her beloved brother, and she herself commemorated him, albeit transporting him from Oxfordshire to Hampshire, in one of her poems, entitled *August Again*, which includes the verse:

> "The heather flings her purple robe
>   Once more upon the hill;
> Beneath a shivering aspen-tree
>   My love lies cold and still;—
> Ah, very deep my Love must sleep,
>   On that far Flemish plain,
> If he does not know the heath-bells blow
>   On the Hampshire hills, again!"

Flora makes occasional references to her younger siblings in her books, but does not build up the detailed picture of them that she does of Edwin.

Neighbours

Flora later wrote that in writing *Lark Rise* she accurately described the people and places she remembered from her childhood, but she has made some significant changes in her depictions of them, perhaps deliberately to make them less readily identifiable, perhaps because she was remembering them many years later, and memory is fallible. However she draws wonderfully detailed pictures. Some can be readily identified, such as Sally and Dick, in real life Sarah and Richard Moss, who were involved in the Juniper Hill riots, although significant details about them have been altered. The pair were recorded in the 1871 census as both being 58, a good deal younger than Flora suggested in her book, though by the time she was ten in 1886 Sally would have been 73. The couple represented for her the old pre-enclosure society, living in more comfortable circumstances than others in the village. Dick was apparently a small, rather withered man who wore a smock-frock (out of fashion by this time), and spent much time tending his big garden. His wife Sally seems to have been a larger than life character who left a lasting impression on the young Flora. She used her character in her writings for the *Catholic Fireside* long before she thought about writing *Lark Rise*. She vividly described Sally and her cottage, giving a rare first hand description of what life was like in a village towards the end of the Victorian era:

" Sally was tall and broad, not fat, but massive, and her large, beamingly good-natured face, with its well-defined moustache and tight, coal-black curls bobbing over each ear, was framed in a white cap frill; for Sally, though still strong and active, was over eighty, and had remained faithful to the fashions of her youth.

She was the dominating partner . . . the house was hers and she carried the purse; but Dick was a willing subject, and enjoyed her

10. Sally and Dick Moss, who owned the largest and best equipped house in the village when Flora was a child. (Oxfordshire Photographic Archive)

dominion over him. It saved him a lot of thinking, and left him free to give all his time and attention to the growing things in his garden.

Old Sally's was a long, low, thatched cottage with diamond-paned windows winking under the eaves and a rustic porch smothered in honeysuckle. Excepting the inn, it was the largest house in the hamlet, and of the two downstair rooms one was used as a kind of kitchen storeroom, with pots and pans and a big red crockery water vessel at one end, and potatoes in sacks and peas and beans spread out to dry at the other. The apple crop was stored on racks suspended beneath the ceiling and bunches of herbs dangled below. In one corner stood the big brewing copper in which Sally still brewed with good malt and hops once a quarter. The scent of the last brewing hung over the place until the next and mingled with apple and onion and dried thyme and sage smells, with a dash of soap-suds thrown in, to compound the aroma which remained in the children's memories for life . . .

The inner room — 'the house', as it was called—was a perfect snuggery, with walls two feet thick and outside shutters to close at night and a padding of rag rugs, red curtains and feather cushions within. There was a good oak, gate-legged table, a dresser with pewter and willow-pattern plates, and a grandfather's clock that not only told the time, but the day of the week as well. It had even once told the changes of the moon . . .

The garden was a large one, tailing off at the bottom into a little field where Dick grew his corn crop. Nearer the cottage were fruit trees, then the yew hedge, close and solid as a wall, which sheltered the bee-hives and enclosed the flower garden. Sally had such flowers, and so many of them, and nearly all of them sweet-scented! Wallflowers and tulips, lavender and sweet william, and pinks and old-world roses with enchanting names— Seven Sisters, Maiden's Blush, moss rose, monthly rose, cabbage rose, blood rose, and, most thrilling of all to the children, a big bush of the York and Lancaster rose, in the blooms of which the rival roses mingled in a pied white and red. It seemed as though all the roses in Lark Rise had gathered together in that one garden. Most of the gardens had only one poor starveling bush or none; but then nobody else had so much of anything as Sally."

Lark Rise to Candleford, pp.76–79

Flora wrote that the house had been built by Sally's grandfather before enclosure, but here she has distorted the facts. Sally herself, the daughter of

John Stephens, who was not a Cottisford man, was born in Helmdon, Northamptonshire, in about 1812 and died in October 1895 aged 83. She came to Cottisford after marrying George Fox, an agricultural labourer, who had built a squatter's cottage in the village in 1847, which he agreed at enclosure to lease for fourteen years. Sarah was a lacemaker and they had one son, John, who was also an agricultural labourer. By the time of the 1861 census Sarah had given up lace making, and had no occupation. At that time Richard Moss, aged 46, an agricultural labourer, was married to Mary, and they had two sons, William and Robert, both agricultural labourers and a daughter Mary Ann. After the deaths of George Fox and Mary Moss Sarah and Richard were married in 1869, so Flora was inaccurate in stating that they had been married for 60 years. It was Richard Moss who owned the cottage, not Sarah, and his father had been one of only four men granted the right of freeholder at enclosure, when his claim to the cottage, with a garden and an acre of land was formally recognised. It is more likely that the items which made the house so comfortable were inherited from his side of the family.

Flora suggested that Sally told her about the village as it had been at the beginning of the 19th century, before enclosure, when the village still stood in the middle of a furzy heath dotted with juniper bushes, boasting only six houses in a ring. But Sally would not have known the village then, although Dick might have done. By this time two new cottages had evidently been added to the original four cottages of the eighteenth century, and gradually more would be built. Again she used Sally as a vehicle to describe how the agricultural labourers had lost much of their ability to earn money in other ways at enclosure, such as by keeping cows, geese and poultry, in addition to the pigs still cosseted in the back gardens. The grazing for these was lost at enclosure, so the wives could no longer make butter to sell. Labourers no longer had the right of cutting furze for firing, and many other advantages were lost. Again, this probably referred to Dick's family rather than Sally's.

As some of the village houses were built as squatters' cottages, without the benefit of architects and professional builders, it is hardly surprising that many only had a short life—Flora came back to visit Juniper later in life, and must have been horrified by what she saw: the roofs of some cottages had fallen in and the only trace of Sally and Dick's was a whitish mark in the corner of a ploughed field.

In *The Peverel Papers* she wrote about 'Old Sally' as a beewife, almost certainly mingling the characters of Sarah Moss and lacemaker Queenie Massey. Sugar was expensive, so keeping bees for their honey was a common alternative among country people, who could also make a little ready money by selling honey and beeswax. The beehives were usually straw beeskeps at this time rather than rectangular wooden hives. The light skeps were weighted down with locally made red earthenware pans:

> " On a three-legged stool beside them their mistress would sit dreaming and dozing for a whole summer day together, a little old woman in a mauve sun-bonnet and plaid shawl who may have dropped straight out of a fairy-tale.
>
> Now and again, in early summer, a loud hubbub would arise in the sleepy garden—a sound of beating and drumming, tinkling and jangling; and then the villagers would smile at each other and say: "Old Sally's bees've a'swarmed"; and anyone near enough would see the old woman rushing wildly backwards and forwards, bonnet strings flying, as she followed the flight of a column of whirling wings, banging all the time with her door key upon whatever pot or pan had come nearest."

The Peverel Papers, p.88

Sally and Queenie shared several attributes, both of them in real life being lacemakers and keeping bees. Queenie and her husband Twister Macey can be found for the first time in Juniper Hill in the 1881 census as Thomas Massey, aged 68, agricultural labourer, born in Launton, and his wife Eliza, aged 71, born in Lower Heyford. They lived in the tiny cottage set almost in front of the End House. Although Eliza cannot have had personal memories of the great period of lace-making in the village, Flora was correct in saying that it had been important. In the 1851 census 19 of the female population of 125 were lacemakers. The invention of the Nottingham lace-making machines devastated the cottage industry of bobbin lace making, which was slow and labour intensive, so by 1861 no lace-makers were listed there in the census.

Flora wrote a vivid description of Queenie:

> "She seemed very old to the children, for she was a little, wrinkled, yellow-faced old woman in a sunbonnet; but she cannot have been nearly as old as Sally ... old Master Macey, commonly called 'Twister', was still able to work part of the time, and they managed to keep their home going."

Lark Rise to Candleford, pp 81-2

11. Queenie Massey, the lacemaker and bee-keeper who lived next door to the Timms family. (Oxfordshire Photographic Archive)

Queenie kept her tiny cottage clean and tidy, but once she had whitened the hearthstone and polished the brass candlesticks, if the weather was fine she would take her lace pillow and low stool out to the beehives and sit there, her face protected by her lilac sunbonnet, and make lace, or doze in the sunshine. Queenie must have started to learn lace-making, probably at a special lace school, when she was about four or five, as children had to start young when their fingers were still very supple, to achieve the speed required to earn money. She would have worked on a big pillow stuffed with straw, using slim bone or wood lace bobbins weighted with bead spangles, perhaps decorated with messages such as '*KISS ME QUICK FOR MOTHER IS COMING*' or '*TAKE THIS SMALL GIFT I FREELY GIVE AND THE LORD PROTECT YOU WHILE YOU LIVE*' probably making the highly-prized Bucks point lace:

12. Queenie would have used a lace pillow and bobbins similar to those used here by Elizabeth Hinks of Fringford. (Oxfordshire Photographic Archive)

"Queenie at her lace-making was a constant attraction to the children. They loved to see the bobbins tossed hither and thither, at random as it seemed to them, every bobbin weighted with its bunch of bright beads and every bunch with its own story, which they had heard so many times that they knew it by heart, how this bunch had been part of a blue bead necklace worn by her little sister who had died at five years old, and this other one had belonged to her mother, and that black one had been found, after she was dead, in a work-box belonging to a woman who was reputed to have been a witch.

There had been a time, it appeared, when lace-making was a regular industry in the hamlet. Queenie, in her childhood, had been 'brought up to the pillow' sitting among the women at eight years old and learning to fling her bobbins with the best of them. They would gather in one cottage in winter for warmth, she said, each one bringing her faggot or shovel of coals for the fire, and there they would sit all day, working, gossiping, singing old songs, and telling old tales till it was time to run home and put on the pots for their husbands' suppers ... In very cold winter weather the lace-makers would have a small earthen pot with a lid, called a 'pipkin', containing hot embers, at which they warmed their hands and feet and sometimes sat upon."

Lark Rise to Candleford, p. 83

Now the laceman no longer called to purchase the hand-made lace and women no longer took it to sell at Banbury Fair.

Queenie managed as best she could, with her husband being such a poor provider. Flora told the story of how she used to collect milk from the farmhouse in Cottisford, which was supposed to be sold at a penny a pint, but people took their own containers and the lax dairymaid just filled them, whatever the size and still charged only a penny. Queenie gradually increased the size of her container until she dared to take a tin cooking boiler. Flora and Edmund were intrigued, suggesting that she could make a good rice pudding with it, and Queenie responded that she never made rice

13. Queenie's Cottage (Banbury Museum)

puddings—all the milk was used to fatten her pig, who was so fat he could hardly see out of his eyes! The family pig was the mainstay of the family diet in those days, and the fatter the meat was, the better they thought it.

Queenie had been married the day Queen Victoria was crowned, and because of that she was taken out of Bicester Workshouse to be chaired round the town on the day of Edward VII's coronation in 1902. She died not long afterwards and was buried in Bicester on 21 August 1902, aged 81, and the parish registers state that she was then living in Back Way, Bicester.

Twister was apparently not over-fond of work, unless it was beating at shoots. He was only 68 in 1881, and probably still working, although Flora says that he had bad rheumatism which forced him to work part time. He was described as:

"... a small thin-legged, jackdaw-eyed old fellow, and dressed in an old velveteen coat that had once belonged to a gamekeeper, with a peacock's feather stuck in the band of his battered old bowler and a red-and-yellow neckerchief knotted under one ear ...

To serve his own purposes, Twister would sometimes pose as a half-wit, but, as the children's father said, he was no fool where his own interests were concerned. He was ready at any time to clown in public for the sake of a pint of beer, but at home he was morose."

Lark Rise to Candleford, p. 85

According to Flora, Twister died one winter as a result of hunting (in great snowstorms) for a boy who was thought to be trapped in a horse and cart in snowdrifts. As it happened the boy had abandoned the horse and cart and escaped home, but Twister is said to have caught pneumonia and died quickly. The truth of the story is uncertain, but Twister is known to have died in Bicester workhouse and was brought back to be buried in Cottisford in 1899, aged 86.

Another identifiable character is Caroline Arless, a lively neighbour who liked to entertain her friends and talk about the novelettes they were reading. Flora described her as being about 45, but young looking with black hair and flashing eyes, who may have had gipsy blood. She was disapproved of by the local women because she was still having children when she was a grandmother, and she did not have a high standard of honesty:

"Ways and means did not trouble her ... One night she would fry steak and onions for supper and make the hamlet's mouth water, another night there would be nothing but bread and lard on her table. When she had money she spent it, and when she had none she got things on credit or went without . . . Her idea of wise spending was to call in a few neighbours of like mind, set them round a roasting fire, and dispatch one of her toddlers to the inn with the beer can . . . She was so charged with sex vitality that with her all subjects of conversation led to it—not in its filthy or furtive aspects, but as the one great central fact of life.

Yet no one could dislike Mrs Arless, however much she might offend their taste and sense of fitness. She was so full of life and vigour and so overflowing with good nature that she would force anything she had upon anyone she thought needed it, regardless of the fact that it was not and never would be paid for."

Lark Rise to Candleford, pp.112–113

She was hauled up several times in the County Court for non-payment of debts, but always managed to persuade the judge that her debt was due to her large family and her generosity, and got away with it.

Caroline was in real life Caroline Ariss, married to Uriah, an agricultural labourer, both born in Tingewick, Buckinghamshire. At the time of the 1881 census, the first in which she appears resident in Juniper, she was 31 and her husband was 36. They had five children living at home: William, aged 12 who had probably left school as he was not listed as a scholar or as a labourer, Mary, aged, 7 and Elisa aged 5 were both at school, and the youngest two, Uriah aged 3 and Joseph aged one, were still at home. Ten years later in 1981 Uriah was listed as a thatcher, his son William was a shepherd and young Uriah, aged 12, was an agricultural labourer. Four more children had been born: Ernest aged 8, Amy (age hidden by an ink blot in the census), Henry aged 4 and Marian aged 2. This fits better with Flora's recollections, so perhaps she was remembering them from this era.

The 'Waggon and Horses'

The pub, called by Flora the 'Waggon and Horses', has in fact always been 'The Fox'. It first appears in the 1871 census, run by Thomas Harris, aged 63, described as publican and grocer, who was born in Gawcott, Buckinghamshire. His wife Frances, who was 50 came from Herefordshire and they had three children: Eliza Mary, aged 9, Aloysius aged 5 and Elizabeth aged 4. A 1-year-old nephew from Scotland was staying with them. Thomas

14. The men of the village spent many convivial evenings in the Fox Inn, which was one of the largest houses in the village and even boasted two four-poster beds. The Harris family who ran it were Catholics.(David Morris)

Harris died in 1875 but Frances appears to have carried on running the pub as in the 1881 census she was described as a widow of 72 and also living at the pub were her 15 year old son Aloysius who had no occupation and their fourteen year old daughter Eliza, plus Joseph Morgan, a tailor of 24, and his wife Elizabeth, 19. Aloysius became a carpenter, and was still living in the village in 1891, when he was 25, with his wife Elizabeth aged 27 and young daughter Winifred.

A valuation had been made of the contents when Thomas Harris died in 1875 (see Appendix 1 for the complete text) which reveals much about the pub and the family. The tap room was furnished with a deal table and twelve Windsor chairs and three corner cupboards, and contained other items such as fifteen spitoons, 23 tumblers, 15 champagne glasses, tea things and kettle and a beer warmer. It seems unlikely that there was much call for champagne in the village! The inn contained a gallon of rum, 35 gallons of 9 per cent beer and 18 gallons of mild.

15. A shooting party outside the Fox Inn, *c*.1890s. (John Watts)

In 1882 another inventory was taken, and by then the taproom was more comfortably furnished with a table and cover, six Windsor chairs, an oak table, a drop-leaf table, sofa, double-front cupboard and writing desk. By 1904 the shop had disappeared and the room was being used as a parlour.

The shop was in a back room in 1875, furnished with a deal counter, scales and weights, an oak table with drawers, mahogany table and writing desk and at the time of the inventory contained bacon, beef suet, lard, sweets and matches for sale. Sugar was probably sold too, as there were sugar nippers in the shop for cutting it up. Perhaps the stock had been run down while Mr. Harris was ill. In the 1882 inventory the only stock for sale appears to have been cheese. Flora wrote that the children used to be sent to the shop to buy candles, treacle and cheese, and commented that after Queen Victoria's Jubilee in 1887 nothing seemed quite the same, and one of the changes was that the shop was selling tins of salmon and of Australian rabbit!

The inn was the largest house in the village, with its own bakehouse, which contained washing trays and tub and a large rectangular lead tray for salting bacon. The field bottles mentioned as being there were probably the costrels or harvest barrels which labourers took into the fields with them filled with beer or cider, to refresh them as they worked. In the hovel were large quantities of potatoes and peas, flour and two stocks of bees with a wheelbarrow and sundry other equipment. The Dutch oven in there was a semi-circular metal contraption from which a joint was hung, which had a dripping tray below to catch melting fat. It was placed in front of the fire and the clock jack wound up so that the joint turned backwards and forwards to cook right through. The concave metal back reflected heat from the open fire to cook the joint more quickly.

There seems to have been no private living room for the publican and his family—they appear to have used the taproom when the pub was not open, as dishes and tea things were kept in there. The house had four well-furnished bedrooms: the main one contained a four-poster bed with feather bed and flock mattress, feather bolster, five pillows, three blankets and a counterpane and other furniture including an oak table, chest of drawers, chairs, night commode, washstand and chest. In the second bedroom was a French bedstead with flock and straw mattresses, in the third bedroom there were two stump bedsteads, and the fourth bedroom contained another four-poster. and volumes of the *Tablet*, a Catholic weekly. Among the items in the loft were four skittles and a ball—perhaps the game was played by the villagers outside the pub. There was also a coal house, and Mr Harris had a sow and six pigs. The presence of four poster beds and flock mattresses suggests that the family were a good deal better off than most of the villagers. The Harris family were Catholic, as Flora wrote, and had to go off to mass each Sunday in a nearby village—hence the presence of the volumes of the Tablet, and the name Aloysius:

"The Catholic minority at the inn was treated with respect, for a landlord could do no wrong, especially the landlord of a free house where such excellent beer was on tap. On Catholicism at large, the Lark Rise people looked with contemptuous intolerance, for they regarded it as a kind of heathenism, and what excuse could there be for that in a Christian country? When, early in life, the end house children asked what Roman Catholics were, they were told they were 'folks as prays to images', and further inquiries elicited the information that they also worshipped the Pope, a bad old man, some said in league with the Devil. Their genuflexions in church and their 'playin' wi' beads' were described as 'monkey tricks'."

Lark Rise to Candleford, pp.213–4

16. Village labourers outside the Fox *c.* 1900. (David Morris)

In December 1882 a valuation was made of the household furniture and effects of the pub when it was transferred to John Harris, presumably a relative. Nothing in the way of stock was listed in the shop, but it must have been revived as in 1891 John Harris aged 44, was described as a licensed victualler, who lived at the pub with his 35 year old wife Ann and their children Mary, 6, Thomas, 5, Kerana, 3 and John 2. They had a servant, Louisa Buckley, aged 12.

The men would meet socially in the pub each evening. The publican would not have got rich on what the men spent, as they could seldom afford more than half a pint each evening, which they sipped to make it last as long as possible—even that sometimes had to be sacrificed when extra feed was needed to fatten the family pig.

The men each had their own places, and women did not join them, nor did children, although they tried to listen to what was going on when they came to buy items from the shop. The men happily discussed politics, told spine-chilling tales, and above all sang folk songs. The younger men knew the popular songs of the day such as *Tommy, Make Room for Your Uncle,* while the middle-aged men specialised in long mournful ballads on topics such as thwarted lovers. All the men could join in songs such as *The Barley-mow*. Thomas Price, who was 59 in 1881, may have been the Master Price who excelled in singing about Lord Lovell:

> "Lord Lovell stood at his castle gate,
> Calming his milk-white steed,
> When up came Lady Nancy Bell
> To wish her lover God-speed ..."

Lark Rise to Candleford, p.72

Flora described Master David Tuffrey, who was indulged because of his great age of 83 by letting him sing about the Outlandish Knight most evenings, as it was the only song he knew, which he had learnt from his grandfather:

> "An outlandish knight, all from the north lands,
> A-wooing came to me,
> He said he would take me to the north lands
> And there he would marry me.
>
> Go fetch me some of your father's gold
> And some of your mother's fee,
> And two of the best nags out of the stable
> Where there stand thirty and three ..."

Lark Rise to Candleford, p.74

The dastardly knight then tried to murder his innocent lady, but she managed to outwit him and he drowned instead of her. David was probably David Tuffrey, actually aged 71 in 1881, a labourer who lived in Juniper with his wife Sarah aged 70.

Flora's early years were spent largely in the hamlet of Juniper, but when she was old enough to go to school the mother village of Cottisford began to feature more in her life.

4

Cottisford: Flora's Fordlow

The tiny village of Cottisford is a mile and a half away from Juniper Hill by road, and it was here that Flora went to school and to church. It was smaller than Juniper, and very different in character, coming under the influence of Eton college who owned much of the land. Although the road is less sunken than a century ago, the buildings are little altered (apart from the conversion of the school and some barns) from those Flora would have seen:

"The village was a little, lost lonely place, much smaller than the hamlet, without a shop, an inn, or a post office, and six miles from a railway station. The little squat church, without spire or tower, crouched back in a tiny churchyard that centuries of use had raised many feet above the road, and the whole was surrounded by tall, windy elms in which a colony of rooks kept up a perpetual cawing. Next came the Rectory, so buried in orchards and shrubberies that only the chimney stacks were visible from the road; then the old Tudor farmhouse with its stone, mullioned windows and reputed dungeon. These, with the school and about a dozen cottages occupied by the shepherd, carter, blacksmith, and a few other superior farm workers, made up the village. Even these few buildings were strung out along the roadside, so far between and so sunken in greenery that there seemed no village at all. It was a standing joke in the hamlet that a stranger had once asked the way to Fordlow after he had walked right through it. The hamlet laughed at the village as 'stuck up'; while the village looked down on 'that gipsy lot' at the hamlet."

Lark Rise to Candleford, pp. 47–8

1. Ordnance Survey map showing Cottisford. Most of the houses are built along the main village street. The village has a long history, as indicated by the medieval fishponds attached to the Manor House, known in the late 19th century as the Manor Farm. The village school is situated on a triangular plot at the crossroads and the houses nearby were model cottages built for agricultural labourers. (Centre for Oxfordshire Studies)

Cottisford has a much longer history than Juniper Hill, being a Saxon village established on the western side of a ford across the Crowell Brook. The earliest forms of the name are 'Wolfheysford' and 'Urlesford', based on a Saxon personal name.

At the Norman Conquest the manor was granted to Hugh de Grant-mesnil who gave control of it to Roger d'Ivry, husband of his daughter Adeline. Adeline in turn granted Cottisford to the abbey of Bec in Normandy, who administered the estates through the priory of Ogbourne in Wiltshire. Bec was an important abbey, being the northern centre of the Cluniac revival; it was Bec who replaced the Saxon church by the present building. The village was at its most prosperous at the end of the 13th century, when there was a flock of 765 sheep. One of Bec's lessees in Cottisford was Sir Roger de Cotesford, three times High Sheriff of Oxfordshire.

The Hundred Years' War with France made the situation of manors attached to alien priories untenable so in 1404 Ogbourne and its manors, including Cottisford, were taken from Bec's ownership and granted by Henry IV to his son John, (later Duke of Bedford), William de St Vaast and Thomas Langley, who became Bishop of Durham, while England was at war with France. In 1438, three years after the death of the Duke of Bedford, Henry VI granted Cottisford to his uncle, Humphrey Duke of Gloucester, revoking his gift in 1441 so that it could be given to his new foundation, Eton College. This gift was confirmed by Edward IV in 1462. Following the practice of Ogbourne, Eton leased out the manor and for sixty years from 1469 it was leased to John Samwell, whose brass of about 1500 can be seen behind the door of Cottisford church, commemorating him, dressed in armour, his wife and their eight sons and five daughters.

The medieval rabbit warren was still important in the 17th century, and there also seem to have been deer on the heath. Succeeding tenants were of less note until in 1739 the manor was leased by Richard Eyre, who had worked for the East India Company for 28 years. The estate was in a neglected state, in 1759 comprising two farms which only brought in £90 and £34 a year, together with a warren worth £8, Mr Eyre's farm and a good house, plus a farm and mill in Fringford, so Eyre had to spend a good deal of money on repairs.

One activity which had died out by the time Flora was born, was Cottisford Races, which ended around the 1820s. The echoes of it remained in village memory as Flora wrote to Leslie Castle that the field found on the right after turning off the main road to go down to Juniper was marked on old maps as 'The Racecourse' and that old people had a tradition about

2. Bryant's map of 1823, drawn when Juniper Hill was too small and insignificant to mention, showing the site of the race course, adjacent to the turnpike road, which disappeared at enclosure. (Centre for Oxfordshire Studies)

races being held there. The races must have caused much excitement locally, with lots of hustle and bustle in the village, with crowds of people arriving to enjoy the races:

"replete as it was then with smug clean shaved squires, parsons, farmers, and traders from the towns and localities of Brackley, Buckingham, and Bicester, arrayed in deep white ties, kerseymere, top boots, and blue or black coats; replete also with young farmers, and farmers' sons, in bright green coats, resplendent with gilt buttons . . . the spruce jocks, in jackets of various colours, the ladies in and on carriages, the grooms, all important in their own eyes, the thickly packed pedestrians, the refreshment booths, the grand stand, the extemporized stables, whose walls were fagots of gorse, and their roofs the open sky, the gambling tents, the thimble riggers, the cards with the names, weights, and colours of the riders, and other publications vended by bawlers, of a nature to tend only to the nourishment of vice and the corruption of youths . . . That long looked for day at the end of March or early in April, the last hunting day but one of the season, converted into a racing day, we will suppose to have arrived. Then was to come off the Farmer's Cup Race, for horses, not thoroughbred, that had regularly hunted with the packs of the Duke of Grafton or Beaufort, or that of Sir Thomas Mostyn, to be ridden by the owners or friendly non-professional riders. This was the great attraction of the day, at least, to the agricultural eye . . . . Nervous enough, and more than enough, looked many of the young farmer riders; albeit confident enough in their own saddles across country, as they emerged from the weighing scale, in tight fitting leather inexpressibles, and flaunting silk jackets and caps, with their sweethearts and sisters, as well as trained jockeys engaged for other races, looking on. Half a dozen false starts were not uncommon; but at last they cry 'they are off', 'they are off' was borne upon the breeze, and the excitement became equal, among a smaller circle, to that of the Londoners on Epsom Downs on a Derby day . . ."

William Wing, Brief Annals of the Bicester Poor Law Union and its Component Parishes, in the County of Oxford and Buckingham, 1879

Although the races were long gone by Flora's time. she did remember Cottisford Feast, an annual event until 1914, which also attracted many people from beyond the village, held on the weekend following 26 August, which is said to commemorate the joy of the villagers at the English victory at the Battle of Crecy on that date in 1346. Flora talks about it taking place on the Sunday and Monday. On the Sunday people, friends and strangers from Brackley and nearby villages, sauntered along the road through Juniper, dressed in their best clothes, and all the families heated their ovens if they had them to provide roast beef and Yorkshire pudding for their visitors. They tried to save a little money from harvest so they could afford to indulge in a little extra alcohol in the pub.

Although it was called Cottisford Feast, and must have originally taken place there before the hamlet developed, by Flora's time it took place largely in Juniper—perhaps because of the proximity of the pub. On the Monday and Tuesday the men had to go back to work, but the women gave

69

tea parties at which the chief delicacy was 'baker's cake', a spicy dough cake flavoured with dried fruit.

Larger village feasts would have had a small fair and several stalls, but only one stall seems to have come to Cottisford Feast by the beginning of the 1880s, the gingerbread stall, with its canvas awning, which sold otherwise seldom obtainable delicacies such as gingerbread babies, striped peppermint humbugs, pink and white rock and various other sweets, including new-fangled items such as chocolate, hitherto unknown in the hamlet:

"A visiting cousin, being fairly well-educated and a great reader, already knew it by name. 'Oh, that's chocolate,' he said off-handedly. 'But don't buy any; it's for drinking. They have it for breakfast in France.' A year or two later, chocolate was a favourite sweet even in a place as remote as the hamlet . . ."

Lark Rise to Candleford, p. 231

Perhaps the cousin was young Johnny Whiting from Twyford, Uncle Tom's son.

3. The family pig was an important member of the household. Most labouring families kept a pig in a sty in the back garden and this provided most of the meat they ate. This pig-sty is attached to one of the model agricultural labourer's cottages near the school.

Life in the Cottisford Flora knew would have been dominated by the Rector, Charles Sawkins Harrison, the family of the squire Edwards Richard Kendal Rousby who lived at Cottisford House and the Waters family who leased the Manor Farm. In the 1881 census there were only twenty-six households in Cottisford (excluding Juniper). Mrs Rousby, a widow, lived at Cottisford House, and two occupiers of land were listed: Joseph Waters at the Manor Farm and Frederick Baines at the Warren. The Rector was assisted by a curate, there were 21 labourers, two gardeners (plus one groom and gardener and one butler and gardener), a blacksmith, mason, carpenter, tailor, schoolmistress, lacemaker and a variety of servants: four general servants, a cook, housemaid, housekeeper, governess and coachman, and there were nine scholars (schoolchildren). This gives a much greater variety of occupations than those found in Juniper, and the description of the men as labourers disguises more specialised occupations such as shepherd and carter. The men lived in tied cottages, which were cheaper than the rented Juniper ones, but gave the men less independence, as if they changed jobs they had to move immediately. Most of the labourers would have worked on the Cottisford farms.

The Farms

The principal farmhouse in Cottisford is the so called 'Tudor farmhouse' described by Flora, which is the Manor Farm. The core of it was probably built by Sir Roger de Cotesford, in the second half of the 14th century, and it was enlarged in the 16th and 17th centuries. The original medieval house had a first floor hall and solar, open to the roof until the 16th century when it was reroofed and a new floor inserted. What Flora thought was a *'reputed dungeon'* was probably the medieval garderobe tower. Some of the medieval windows have been reused in later portions of the house. The farm in Flora's time belonged to the Earl of Effingham, owner of Tusmore House.

A sale catalogue of 1944 shows the extent of the farmhouse, which was probably little changed from when Flora had known it, apart from the addition of electricity and some mod cons:

"The attractive Stone-built Manor Farmhouse with the original stone-mullioned windows . . . fitted with electric light and modern conveniences, contains Accommodation: Five bedrooms, Dressing Room and two Attics, Bathroom and Airing Cupboard (with hot water from an independent boiler in the kitchen) and lavatory.

Lot 2.

THE

COTTISFORD PART

OF THE ESTATE,

CONSISTING OF A SUPERIOR

Stone-built & Slated Farm Residence,

Containing Parlour, Sitting Room, and Kitchen; Cellar, Pantry, Dairy, Brewhouse, 5 Bed-rooms, and 1 Attic. The Premises comprise Granary, Stabling for 20 Cart Horses, three-stall Nag Stable, 3 Barns, 2 Wagon Hovels, Cow-house, Chaff-house, Hen-house, Piggery, Yards, Garden, &c., and

616A. 1R. 19P.

OF ARABLE AND PASTURE LAND,

(CHIEFLY ARABLE,)

DIVIDED INTO THE FOLLOWING INCLOSURES:

As copied from the Tithe Commutation Plan, dated 10th of May 1856.

No. on Plan.	Description of Lands and Premises.	Cultivation.	A.	R.	P.
41	Home Field Allotment	Arable	13	0	38
42	Two Cottages, Gardens and Allotment of Land.......................	——	6	3	30
43	The Heath Allotment	——	35	1	24
44	Knights House Allotment	——	8	0	8
45	Ditto	——	6	2	37
46	Fox Cover Allotment	——	17	0	9
48	Woods House Allotment	——	26	2	14
49	Barn and Yard		0	1	20
49a	Old Driftway		1	3	36
51	Old Freeboard		1	1	0
52	Fox Cover Allotments	Arable	11	3	32
53	Cow Ground Allotments	——	16	0	18
54	Great East Allotment	——	121	2	6
54a	Reserved for Building		2	0	0
55	Great South Allotment	Arable	101	2	35
56	Great West Allotment.............	——	190	2	30
77	Mount Close	——	5	3	37
78	Rick Yard........................		0	0	39
90	Pond Piece Allotment..............	Arable	15	3	19
79	Dove House Piece	——	14	0	5
103	Sanfoin Ground	Grass	12	1	11
106	Rick Yard........................		0	1	34
106a	Allotment from Waste.............		0	1	30
107	Homestead, Garden, Yards, Stables, &c.		1	1	3
108	Garden		0	2	16
110	Moat Close	Meadow	2	0	16
43b	Cottage and Garden		0	0	29
43c	Ditto		0	0	35
43d	Three Cottages and Gardens		0	1	30
101	Five Cottages and Gardens		0	1	26
102	The Kennels.....................		0	0	32
	Total. Acres		**616**	**1**	**19**

Of which Four of the Cottages (part of No. 101) are let to punctual tenants at £15 per annum; one other Cottage, part of No. 101, and the Kennels, No. 102, in hand; and the remainder of the property described in the above particulars let to Mr. RICHARD WOODS, a most respectable yearly tenant,

At £430 per annum,

Exclusive of £81 2s. 6d. tithe rent charge paid by the Tenant to the Rector.

ALSO THE UNDERMENTIONED

Cottages with Gardens, situate at Juniper Hill,

IN THE PARISH OF COTTISFORD, and not shown on the Plan,

Let on Lease for Fourteen Years from Michaelmas 1853, at the following Rents.

4. Extract from the sale catalogue when the Manor Farm was sold in 1853, listing the pre-enclosure fields attached to the Manor Farm. (Centre for Oxfordshire Studies)

Ground Floor: Three reception Rooms, Kitchen (fitted with Triplex Range and an independent boiler), Cloak-room with lavatory and Scullery."

Sale Catalogue, Cottisford Manor Farm, Monday May 8th 1944,
Auctioneers Messrs Stace and Foot, Brackley.

The catalogue goes on to describe the "well laid out Kitchen Garden" and the range of farm buildings, which comprised:

"Nag Stable for three horses with Harness Room adjoining and loft over.

Cow Stall with concrete floor and standing for nine cows.

Seven bay open Cow Hovel opening into an enclosed Yard and sur-rounded by the Cart Stable for seven horses with loft over, Barn with concrete floor.

Large Barn opening on to the main road with Loft over with six wood-partitioned Cornbins to accommodate 250 or so quarters of Wheat and automatically fed by a blast Elevator from the Drier.

Eight-bay enclosed Cow Hovel with Loose Box adjoining and four-bay Implement Hovel.

Loose Boxes, Cow Stall and standing for cows.

Garage. Detached four-bay Implement Hovel.

Various Outbuildings.

Range of six brick-built pigsties, fitted with water troughs and Feed-house adjoining, opening on to another enclosed Crew Yard with five-bay open Cow Hovel.

The Farmhouse and Buildings have a continuous supply of water from the Wind-pump in the Home Paddock and the pump is adapt-able for engine power if required at short notice."

The land was said to be in good heart, especially suited for breeding sheep, growing barley and wheat and sugar beet. (In the late 19th century the prin-cipal crops were corn and turnips with much meadowland and in the 1880s there were about 800 sheep). Perhaps as important to any prospective new owner was the hunting potential:

"Good hunting is available in the immediate district, being in the heart of the Bicester country and within easy reach of the Grafton, Heythrop and Whaddon Chase hunts.

The Estate is noted for its partridge drives and the Game has been preserved for many years and maintained by a keeper."

This ties in with the description Flora gives, about the farm being several farms combined, extending beyond the parish boundaries. She wrote that there were meadows around the farm for the carthorses and a few milking cattle. The main crops were corn, especially wheat, and root crops, supplemented by hay, sainfoin and rye. Many of the farm buildings Flora knew are still there, although the barns, with enormous doors which the blue and yellow painted farm wagons loaded with hay could be driven through, have been converted to housing.

Joseph Waters, the farmer Flora knew, had come to Cottisford in the 1860s, and had farmed several different holdings over the years. He only lived at the Tudor farmhouse from 1882–91, then he went to Home Farm, Shelswell. While at the Manor Farm he farmed more land than anyone else locally, renting some land from the Tusmore Estate and some from Eton

5. The core of the Manor House, now known as Manor Farm, was built in the 14th century, probably by Sir Roger de Cotesford, and has been added to over the centuries. The tenant in Flora's time was Joseph Waters, the principal farmer in the parish. (Oxfordshire Photographic Archive)

College, to a total of about 1400 acres. In 1871 when he lived in an un-named house in Cottisford he employed 34 men, 20 boys and 5 women on the 1200 acres he farmed. He was then aged 38, and had been born in Fringford. His wife Mary, from London, was 34 and they had one servant, Mary Jane Golder aged 16 from Stoke Lyne. Ten years later there were three children at home: Ellen aged 7, George aged 4 and William aged 3, Mary had died shortly after their son William was born in 1879, so the family were looked after by a housekeeper, Elizabeth Lepper, aged 48 and a governess, Franie Mobbs aged 29.

Again Flora has made her character older than in real life. She described how the labourers came to the farmhouse every week to receive their wages personally from Joseph Waters:

> "On Friday evening, when work was done, the men trooped up to the farmhouse for their wages. These were handed out of a window to them by the farmer himself and acknowledged by a rustic scraping of feet and pulling of forelocks. The farmer had grown too old and too stout to ride horseback, and, although he still made the circular tour of his land in his high dogcart every day, he had to keep to the road, and pay-day was the only time he saw many of his men. Then, if there was cause for complaint, was the time they heard of it. 'You, there! What were you up to in Causey Spinney last Monday, when you were sup-posed to be clearing the runnels?' was a type of complaint that could always be countered by pleading. 'Call o' Nature, please, sir.' . . . But, just as often, it would be: 'There, Boamer, there you are my lad, a bright and golden half-sovereign for you. Take care you don't go spending it all at once1' or an enquiry about some wife in childbed or one of the ancients' rheumatism. He could afford to be jolly and affable: he paid poor old Monday Morning to do his dirty work for him.
>
> Apart from that he was not a bad-hearted man and had no idea he was sweating his labourers."
>
> *Lark Rise to Candleford*, pp. 60–1

Waters died in 1901, and his obituary in the *Banbury Guardian* on 24 Octo-ber described him: "His many acts of courtesy, and kindness, his genial dis-position, his strict sense of justice, and his straightforward manner of dealing, endeared him to the parishioners." It is difficult to say who 'Monday Morning', the farm bailiff, could have been, as the last farm bailiff recorded in the census returns was James Tebby in 1861, long before Flora was born.

The history of the area and the land use was encapsulated in the field names, which were shown on the 1855 Tithe Map of Cottisford, including: Drying Close, Ozier Bed, the Pond, Race Course Allotment (recalling Cottisford Races), Ox pasture piece, the Great Warren (where rabbits would have been bred in the middle ages), Great Sheep Pen Ground, Butcher's Meadow, Priests's Close, Dove House Piece, Old Driftway, Moat Close (the manor farm was probably originally defensively moated). Some of these tie up with names Flora remembered:

> "The field names gave the clues to the fields' history. Near the farmhouse, 'Moat Piece', 'Fishponds', 'Duffus Piece', 'Kennels', and 'Warren Piece' spoke of a time before the Tudor house took the place of another and older establishment. Farther on, 'Lark Hill', 'Cuckoos' Clump', 'The Osiers', and 'Pond Piece' were named after natural features, while 'Gibbard's Piece' and 'Blackwell's' probably commemorated otherwise long-forgotten former occupants. The large new fields round the hamlet had been cut too late to be named and were known as 'The Hundred Acres', 'The Sixty Acres', and so on, according to their acreage. One or two of the ancients persisted in calling one of these 'The Heath' and another 'The Racecourse'."
>
> *Lark Rise to Candleford*, p. 52

Long before *Lark Rise to Candleford* was begun, Flora commented on field-names, remembering back to her childhood in Juniper, in *The Peverel Papers*. She regretted that field names were becoming obsolete:

> "Some of these names explained themselves. 'Charlcroft's' was an echo of the reign of a once important local family. 'Lark's Lease'—poor in soil and rich in skylark's song, though at least two centuries had passed since it was named on that account. Loam Pits, Pond Piece, Sanfoin, and Forty Acres were plain straightforward names. But what could be made of Duffus Piece?'"

Some clues to the mystery of Duffus Piece were found in large stone blocks clustered in one corner of the field, revealing that there had once been a building—the dovehouse. This was important for breeding doves for the table in the middle ages, when the flesh of doves counted as fish, and could be eaten on 'fish days'. Flora went on to weave a fantasy about the manor

6. Horseman with his team, *c.* 1900 (John Watts)

7. Agricultural labourers taking a break for refreshments after building a hayrick at Fringford Mill. (John Watts)

house near the ruined dovecote, describing the young squire who had been killed by tripping on his spur running downstairs to go hunting many years before, and how his now ninety year old widow lived in seclusion in the house. Flora wrote that she found an excuse to go to the dairy attached to the house during a milk shortage, and was amazed to see a strange circular building in the courtyard, with little 'doorways' in the walls. She found an imperious old woman who answered her enquiry by telling her that the dairy was "round the corner by the Duffus", and it was explained to her that Duffus was a dove-house. She was obviously fascinated by the way that the old field names revealed snippets about the history of the area.

The other Cottisford farm, entitled Warren Farm, was tenanted in 1881 by Frederick Baines, aged 35 from Souldern, with his wife Martha, aged 33, and their six children, who did not have a living-in servant.

Most of the labourers in Cottisford and Juniper Hill would have worked for these two men, although some may have had to travel outside the parish to find work. The 1871 and 1881 censuses list the men just as labourers, but in 1891 we can find out more about them. In Cottisford specialist workers such as an agricultural milkman, a horse waggoner and shepherd were mentioned. As superior workers they received slightly higher wages, and usually lived in tied cottages close to their work. Most of the boys, when they left school at the age of about 12, would become farm labourers, many of them having already done odd jobs around the farm for years already.

Their work was hard, and they had to be out in all weathers, protected only by crude sacking to form a hooded cloak when it rained, working for meagre wages, but on the whole they were healthy.

It was at harvest time that the men had to work the longest hours, to cut the precious grain while the weather held, and this was the last generation of men doing it by hand, before the advent of farm machinery - some of that used locally probably made by the famous firm of Samuelson's of Banbury. They upheld the traditions of generations:

" . . . they still kept up the old country custom of choosing as their leader the tallest and most highly skilled man amongst them, who was then called 'King of the Mowers'. For several harvest in the 'eighties they were led by the man known as Boamer. He had served in the Army and was still a fine well-set up young fellow, with flashing teeth and a skin darkened by fiercer than English suns.

With a wreath of poppies and bindweed trails around his wide rush-plaited hat, he led the band down the swathes as they mowed, and decreed when and for how long they should halt for 'a breather' and what drinks they had from the yellow stone jar they kept under the hedge in a shady corner of the field. They did not rest often or long: for every morning they set themselves to accomplish an amount of work in the day that they knew would tax all their powers till long after sunset."

Lark Rise to Candleford, p. 235

Each year the farmer provided a harvest home dinner for his men. This could be a poignant occasion, for labourers were often employed on a yearly contract, dispersing after harvest for a few days well earned rest, then attending the nearest hiring fair to find a new job, so it might be the last time that that particular group of people got together. Many names recur through the decades at Juniper and Cottisford, but other names come and go, so there was a certain turnover of men.

8. A group of labourers standing by a traction engine, probably at Shelswell Park. (Baroness von Maltzahn). Flora commented that machines were gradually taking over from men in the fields: "Machinery was just coming into use on the land. Every autumn appeared a pair of large traction engines, which posted on each side of a field drew a plough across by means of a cable." (*Lark Rise to Candleford*, p. 53)

The harvest supper was often the best meal the labourers had all year, a welcome change from their usual diet of meat from the family pig and vegetables grown on their allotments, supplemented by bread. Breakfast was seldom eaten that morning, to leave more room for the feast.

" And what a feast it was! Such a bustling in the farmhouse kitchen for days beforehand; such a boiling of hams and roasting of sirloins; such a stacking of plum puddings, made by the Christmas recipe; such a tapping of eighteen-gallon casks and baking of plum loaves would astonish those accustomed to the appetites of today. By noon the whole parish had assembled, the workers and their wives and children to feast and the sprinkling of the better-to-do to help with the serving. The only ones absent were the aged bedridden and their attendants, and to them, the next day, portions, carefully graded in daintiness according to their social standing, were carried by the children from the remnants of the feast. A plum pudding was considered a delicate compliment to an equal of the farmer, slices of beef or ham went to the 'bettermost poor'; and a ham-bone with plenty of meat left upon it or part of a pudding or a can of soup to the commonalty.

Long tables were laid out of doors in the shade of a barn, and soon after twelve o'clock the cottagers sat down to the good cheer, with the farmer carving at the principal table, his wife with her tea urn at another, the daughters of the house and their friends circling the tables with vegetable dishes and beer jugs, and the grandchildren in their stiff, white, embroidered frocks, dashing hither and thither to see that everybody had what they required. . . .

After the dinner there were sports and games, then dancing in the home paddock until twilight, and when, at the end of the day, the farmer, carving indoors for the family supper, paused with knife poised to listen to the last distant 'Hooray!' and exclaimed, 'A lot of good chaps! A lot of good chaps, God bless 'em!' both he and the cheering men were sincere, however mistaken."

Lark Rise to Candleford, pp. 237–8

Flora again looked behind the surface enjoyment of the occasion to its implications, here giving it as her father's opinion, that of an outsider, as he was not employed by the farmer:

"It did not do to look beneath the surface. Laura's father, who did not

81

come into the picture, being a 'tradesman' and so not invited, used to say that the farmer paid his men starvation wages all the year and thought he made it up to them by giving that one good meal. The farmer did not think so, because he did not think at all, and the men did not think so either in that day; they were too busy enjoying the food and the fun."

Lark Rise to Candleford, p.238

The wages paid were low, even by Oxfordshire standards, so the labourers would have had some cause for complaint. As Joseph Waters' wife died in 1879, she could only have presided over the dinners when Flora was very young, so perhaps the housekeeper took her place at later occasions.

The Church

The little church, built in the thirteenth century and much restored by Charles Buckeridge in 1861, has a particular charm. It is tiny, consisting of a nave and chancel. The Rousbys of Cottisford House had the east and west windows ornamented with their own diaphane work in 1860 and one window was dedicated by the Sawkins Harrisons to two of their children in 1870. It is loved and well-tended by the villagers, and has become a place of pilgrimage for lovers of *Lark Rise to Candleford*. The interior has changed, with a different arrangement of pews, whitewashed walls instead of the roughcast stone of Flora's time, the addition of an organ, and no more unpleasant smells from the crypt!

"The Squire's and clergyman's families had pews in the chancel, with backs to the wall on either side, and between them stood two long benches for the schoolchildren, well under the eyes of authority. Below the steps down into the nave stood the harmonium, played by the clergyman's daughter, and round it was ranged the choir of small schoolgirls. Then came the rank and file of the congregation, nicely graded, with the farmer's family in the front row, then the Squire's gardener and coachman, the schoolmistress, the maidservants, and the cottagers, with the Parish Clerk at the back to keep order."

Lark Rise to Candleford, p.210

Flora and Edwin sat in a pew half way down the nave, probably close to

9. Cottisford Church, although small, is full of character. Edmund Timms is commemorated on the brass war memorial. (Oxfordshire Photographic Archive)

where the war memorial has been placed on the wall. In 1995 a plaque was unveiled commemorating Flora herself.

A largely new Rectory had been built in Cottisford in 1821 by Peake of Fringford, for T. W. Champneys, who lived at Fulmer in Buckinghamshire. A datestone reading 1618 or 1619 can be found at the back of the house, perhaps revealing the date of the earlier one. The tithe barn behind the Rectory has a datestone recording its restoration in 1651. When Charles Sawkins Harrison, who had studied for his M.A. at Durham University, came to Cottisford in 1853 he lived there, and spent £400 enlarging the house. In 1861 he was aged 45, and lived at the rectory with his 38 year old wife Margaret and their children Grace, aged 9, Richard aged 8, Amy aged 7, Edmund aged 4, Clement aged 3, George aged 2 and infant Basil. To help in the house they had 21 year old governess Joanna Goodall, 40 year old Martha Mortley, cook, 23 year old nurse Jane Clayton, house maid Emily Austin aged 18 and nurse girl Eliza Mansfield aged 14. By 1881 his wife Margaret had died, and his elder daughter Grace, then aged 29, still lived with him and helped him with his parish work.

10. Charles Sawkins
Harrison, Rector of Cottis-
ford from 1853–96, who was
rechristened Rev. Ellison in
Lark Rise to Candleford.
(Cottisford Parochial
Church Council)

Harrison was a well-known figure to Flora and Edwin, as he came into the school at ten o'clock each morning to teach the children scripture:

"He was a clergyman of the old school; a commanding figure, tall and stout, with white hair, ruddy cheeks and an aristocratically beaked nose, and he was as far as possible removed by birth, education, and worldly circumstances from the lambs of his flock. He spoke to them from a great height, physical, mental and spiritual. 'To order myself lowly and reverently before my betters' was the clause he underlined in the Church Catechism, for had he not been divinely appointed pastor and master to those little rustics and was it not one of his chief duties to teach them to realise this? As a man, he was kindly disposed—a giver of blankets and coals at Christmas, and of soup and milk puddings to the sick."

Lark Rise to Candleford, p. 179

He regularly preached on the duty of regular church-going, forgetting that his congregation did that already, and those to whom he wanted his message to go were not there to hear it! He also imprinted on their minds the importance of the social order and that each one should be happy to stay in his own niche. He worked his way regularly round the parish, visiting each family at least once each year, but was not always a welcome visitor, as the house had to be rapidly tidied as news came of his approach.

He died in 1896. His daughter Grace actively helped him in the parish. She had the responsibility for taking care of the box of baby clothes lent out to mothers who needed it, with its half dozen of everything: "tiny shirts, swathes, long flannel barrows, nighties, and napkins", which she made and repaired between each use. She prepared little packets as welcome gifts for the new mothers, with tea, sugar and patent oats to make gruel. She helped the mothers find places as servants for their daughters, by asking round to see where there were local vacancies, and if necessary placing advertisements in the *Church Times* or the *Morning Post*. She also visited the hamlet families often, carefully visiting each in turn lest any get jealous, not realising that to many her visits were unwanted:

" Considering her many kindnesses to the women, she might have been expected to be more popular than she was. None of them welcomed her visits. Some would lock their doors and pretend to be out; others would rattle their teacups when they saw her coming, hoping she would say, as she sometimes did, 'I hear you are at tea, so I won't come in.'

The only spoken complaint about her was that she talked too much. 'That Miss Ellison, she'd fair talk a donkey's hind leg off,' they would say; but that was a failing they tolerated in others, and one to which they were not averse in her, once she was installed in their best chair and some item of local gossip was being discussed.

Perhaps at the root of their unease in her presence was the subconscious feeling of contrast between her lot and theirs. Her neat little figure, well corseted in; her clear high-pitched voice, good clothes, and faint scent of lily-of-the-valley perfume put them, in their workaday garb and all blowsed from their cooking or water-fetching, at a disadvantage."

Lark Rise to Candleford, pp. 221–2

She was friendly with Emma, Flora's mother, whom it was said she had known from birth, and at the time when Emma worked at Fewcott Rectory. Flora was incorrect in saying that she was the only daughter, but she was the eldest, and therefore the task of caring for her father may naturally have devolved on her.

Flora mentions the curates—'Mr Alport' the "big, fat-faced young man, who had been a medical student", keeping a dispensary at his lodging, may perhaps have been Samuel Luffman, aged 26, who lived with his wife Maria in Dog Kennel Cottage in 1881. 'Mr Marley', the old man with a grey beard, who was an Anglo-Catholic, may have been William R. Almond, aged 50, who is found in the 1891 census, lodging with labourer William Cross.

11. Flora has recently been commemorated with a plaque in the church.

Cottisford House

Next to the church stands Cottisford House—there have been several big houses on the site over the centuries, the current one being built about 1700 by Laurence Lord, as a square building of coursed rubble decorated with ashlar quoin stones, with a hipped roof and attic dormers. At one time there was a lane with several cottages between the church and the house, but Squire William Turner who held Cottisford House at the beginning of the 19th century decided to use the £20,000 brought by his Welsh wife Maria Meares on their marriage in 1825 to enlarge the house and extend the grounds. As part of this refurbishment he demolished the cottages, closed the lane and laid out fine pleasure gardens, rebuilding the cottages well away from the house. He drastically overspent on his improvements, and was unable to enjoy the fruits of his labour: he had to flee to Belgium to escape his creditors, dying in Bruges in 1836.

The Rousbys were the family that Flora knew, although she rechristened them the Bracewells. In 1871 Edwards Rousby, gentleman, aged 52, was living at the house with his wife Louisa, aged 41, and their daughters Edith, 16, and Josephine, 13. Their unmarried son Edwards Richard Kendal Rousby purchased the house from Eton College in 1885 and in the 1891 census was living there aged 34, with his mother, their cook Mary Langley, aged 49, from Clewer, Buckinghamshire and two domestic servants, Jane Clist, aged 22, from Batripp, Somerset and Elizabeth Higgs, aged 19, from West Hanney, Berks. They performed the role of squire and family in the village. After Mrs Rousby was widowed she carried on visiting the village school to examine the girls' needlework,

" . . . a haughty, and still handsome old dame in a long flowing, pale-grey silk dustcloak and small close-fitting black bonnet, with two tiny King Charles spaniels on a leash.

12. Cottisford House seen after the improvements made by William Turner in the early 19th century. When Flora knew it as a child it was the home of the Rousby family whom she called the Bracewells. (Oxfordshire Photographic Archive)

It would be almost impossible for any one born in this century to imagine the pride and importance of such small country gentlepeople in the 'eighties. As far as was known, the Bracewells were connected with no noble family; they had but little land, kept up but a small establishment, and were said in the village and hamlet to be 'poor as crows'. Yet, by virtue of having been born into a particular caste and of living in the 'big house' of the parish, they expected to reign over their poorer neighbours and to be treated by them with the deference due to royalty."

Lark Rise to Candleford, pp. 194–5

Flora wrote that 'Mrs Bracewell' had been brought up during the Regency, but in fact she was born in 1831. She commented that she was generous in her way, despite her shortage of money, providing for two old women, organising soup for the 'deserving poor' in the winter and providing a special tea and magic-lantern show for the schoolchildren at Christmas.

In the 1860s there were two gamekeepers employed in Cottisford, and one in 1871, indicating that the male members of the family would have enjoyed shooting, and presumably hunting. The Rousbys did not maintain a large household: living in the house at the time of the 1861 census were a ladies' maid (who was a visitor), a cook, a nurse and a housemaid, and in 1871, when they had two daughters, Edith, aged 16, and Josephine, aged 13, living at home, they had a governess, a cook, a housemaid and a children's maid. The Rousbys probably also employed Henry Price, aged 37, who described himself as a groom and gardener. When she was widowed, Mrs Rousby obviously decided that she needed a man about the house, so she employed 65 year old James Baines as butler and gardener, plus a cook, housemaid and general servant. Baines was married, but seems to have lived at Cottisford House, as his wife Charlotte who lived in a cottage in Cottisford described herself as butler's wife and head of her household in the census. Thomas Mansfield, aged 78, who was described as a groom and coachman, probably also worked for her.

The School

The triangle of land at the crossroads was allocated for a school at the time of enclosure in 1854, and the little school, paid for by Charles Sawkins Harrison, with grants from Eton College and the National Society for the Education of the Poor in the Principles of the Established Church, opened in 1856. Flora described it minutely:

"Fordlow National School was a small grey one-storied building standing at the cross-roads at the entrance to the village. The one large classroom which served all purposes was well-lighted with several windows, including the large one which filled the end of the building which faced the road. Beside, and joined on to the school, was a tiny two-roomed cottage for the schoolmistress, and beyond that a play-ground with birch trees and turf, bald in places, the whole being enclosed within white-painted palings . . . The school . . . had a lobby with pegs for clothes, boys' and girls' earth-closets, and a backyard with fixed wash-basins, although there was no water laid on. The water supply was contained in a small bucket, filled every morning by the old woman who cleaned the schoolroom, and every morning she grumbled because the children had been so extravagant that she had to 'fill 'un again'.

Lark Rise to Candleford, p. 177

13. Cottisford School, which opened in 1856, was built at the crossroads to cater for about 45 pupils and one teacher. (Oxfordshire Photographic Archive)

As the old log books of Cottisford School have disappeared without trace, there is little direct information about the school in Flora's time apart from what she has so vividly written. There were about forty five pupils, varying in age from about 4 to 14, although most children left school at 12. All had to be taught by the one teacher in the one classroom, helped only by untrained pupil-teachers chosen from amongst the elder children. The first teacher Flora knew was Susannah Holmyard, who she said had been at the school since the mid 1860s, and had been engaged to the squire's head gardener for most of that time:

> "She was at that time, about forty, and was a small neat little body with a pale, slightly pock-marked face, snaky black curls hanging down to her shoulders, and eyebrows arched into a perpetual enquiry. She wore in school stiffly starched, holland aprons with bibs, one embroidered in red one week, and one with blue the next, and was seldom seen without a posy of flowers pinned on her breast and another tucked into her hair."
>
> *Lark Rise to Candleford*, p. 178

14. The interior of Cottisford School with the teacher's desk on the right and the rows of benches for the children. The room was heated by one turtle stove, so must have become very cold in winter. c.1905. (Oxfordshire Photographic Archive)

Susannah Holmyard was not the first teacher, as Ann Walter, aged 20 from Bicester, held that post in 1861. Susannah came in 1867 as an untrained teacher, earning only £27 10s a year in the early 1870s, mitigated slightly by the fact that she could live rent free in the tiny cottage attached to the school. She worked for her teacher's certificate by external examination, gaining it in 1872, which raised her salary to £32 4s a year. She was much younger than Flora suggested, being 34 in 1881. Henry Tebby, her fiancé, (called Tenby in *Lark Rise to Candleford*) was 28 in 1881, and described as a servant in 1871 rather than a gardener. Ten years later he had advanced to being a gardener, and lived on his own. They married in April 1885, when Mrs Rousby graciously acted as a witness. While Susannah, as a married woman, had to give up work, Henry carried on working as gardener at Cottisford House. They did not have children.

None of the teachers after that stayed so long. Flora called the next teacher Matilda Annie Higgs. She was a progressive teacher who tried to treat the children as friends, but by doing this disastrously lost all authority over them:

"They hid her cane, filled her inkpot with water, put young frogs in her desk, and asked her silly, unnecessary questions about their work. When she answered them, they all coughed in chorus."

Lark Rise to Candleford, p. 185

This behaviour often reduced the poor woman to tears and it was obvious that the situation could not continue indefinitely. It was when the Rector arrived at the school in time to witness a pitched battle between some of the older boys in the classroom that the end came. He easily restored order, but 'Miss Higgs' had to go. For a while Mrs Tebby was recalled, until 'Miss Shepherd' was appointed. She was much older, but again not strong on keeping discipline, but she kept things going. She obviously liked Flora, and must have got to know her well, as Flora stayed on a year longer than most of the other pupils, and helped her teach the younger ones. Once, after the Bishop had come to consecrate an extension to the churchyard, 'Miss Shepherd', disappointed at not having been invited back to the Rectory for tea, instead invited Flora to tea in her little cottage attached to the school. She had transformed the tiny one up one down cottage to suit 'artistic taste', with a green serge table-cloth hiding the old deal table, cushions and anti-maccassars, and masses of fashionable decorations and examples of her craft work such as wool-work, hanging pincushions and letter racks, plus Japanese fans, pictures and photographs, covering the walls.

Apart from the daily scripture lessons, taught by Mr. Sawkins Harrison, the main subjects for the children were reading, writing and arithmetic, while each afternoon the girls were taught sewing—as most of them would end up in service it was important to be able to darn and mend, and be able to embroider cross-stitch names on clothes, if they wanted to rise above menial duties. Flora loathed the sewing and commented wryly that while the other girls were busy making their pinafores she was still struggling with her grubby, blood-stained hemming strip. Writing lessons were used to inculcate morality as well as teach a copperplate hand, with maxims such as 'A fool and his money are soon parted'. Essays were set to teach composition and spelling. Other subjects were taught on a more informal basis:

> "History was not taught formally; but history readers were in use containing such picturesque stories as those of King Alfred and the cakes, King Canute commanding the waves, the loss of the White Ship, and Raleigh spreading his cloak for Queen Elizabeth.
>
> There were no geography readers, and, excepting what could be gleaned from the descriptions of different parts of the world in the ordinary readers, no geography was taught. But, for some reason or other, on the walls of the schoolroom were hung splendid maps: The World, Europe, North America, South America, England, Ireland, and Scotland. During long waits in class for her turn to read, or to have her copy or sewing examined, Laura would gaze on these maps until the shapes of the countries, with their islands and inlets became photographed on her brain. Baffin Bay and the land around the poles were especially fascinating to her."
>
> *Lark Rise to Candleford*, p. 180

Flora had been taught the rudiments of reading by her father before she went to school, but was too shy to tell the teacher, who on finding she could not recite the alphabet decided she could not read either. She did not enjoy arithmetic, but must have been reasonably good with figures to be able to work in the post office in later life.

The day the children dreaded most was the annual visit of Her Majesty's Inspector, who came to examine each child. Their results materially affected the future funding of the school, as if they performed badly, the funds would be reduced for the next year. The Inspector was an elderly clergy-

man, of "autocratic demeanour and scathing judgement", and little understanding of children, confusing them utterly by enunciating the punctua-
tion as well as the words in giving dictation. A School Inspector appears
again in Flora's novel *Still Glides the Stream*, where the heroine is Charity,
who is a pupil teacher who very much wants to become a teacher:

15. Needlework was taught to the girls each afternoon, and was the bane of Flora's
life: while the other girls were busy stitching pinafores she was still struggling with
her first blood–bespattered hemming strip. The needlework illustrated here,
which is similar to that done in Cottisford School, was submitted by Cherwell
British Schools, Banbury, for the Oxford Prize Scheme for Needlework. Each
sample is labelled with the name, age and standard of the pupil. (Oxfordshire
Museums Service)

"The time of the annual visit of Her Majesty's Inspector of Schools was drawing near and she had extra lessons of her own to prepare, as well as to help Miss Fowkes coach some of the backward pupils . . . That year, too, she had fears and apprehensions on her own behalf, for the time of her probation as monitress had expired and upon the decision of the great man her whole future depended. For it was he, and only he, who could accept or reject her application for the advanced post of pupil teacher. but for her personally all went well on the day of judgement.

Mr Findlater was a learned man, an historian, with a leaning to the already becoming-less-popular Right. It happened that Charity's history paper dealt with the events leading up to the Civil War, and, unwittingly, she gained her examiner's favour by supporting the royal cause. At the end of her *viva voce*, he grunted, 'Very creditable', and, instead of going away and leaving her in suspense, as he often did with such candidates, he told her at once that the appointment was hers. After he had gone, Miss Fowkes kissed and congratulated her upon 'passing with honours', and she bounded home to tell her parents the good news with her head in the air. It was years later, when she came to read Mr Findlater's *England in the Seventeenth Century* that she recognised the working of Chance."

Still Glides the Stream, pp. 123–4

It is possible that the Inspector Flora is referring to here was the Rev. James Blomfield, a learned man who was Rector of Launton, and rural dean of Bicester, who wrote extensively about the local history of the area in the 1880s and 1890s although not so far as is known about England in the 17th century.

As the early log books have disappeared it is not possible to see what the Inspector thought of the school. However some of the reports of the Diocesan Inspector, who was a much more welcome visitor, who actually encouraged the children instead of terrifying them, have been preserved. On the day assigned for the visit the teacher would dress in her best and watch while he asked the class Scripture questions and gave them a written essay on some biblical topic. Mr Sawkins Harrison had done his work well, and the children were easily able to answer.

Flora won the Diocesan prize in 1888, inspired by the subject of the life of Moses. The Inspector's Report for that year read:

"The Religious Instruction has been painstaking and the children are evidently interested in their work. The 1st Class especially passed a very creditable examination, both in Holy Scripture and Catechism— Catechism, passages of Holy Scripture etc. were very well repeated and the written work was, on the whole, good.

Diocesan Prize: Flora Timms

Commended Isabel Blaby, Sarah A. Cripps, Charles E. Adams"

Oxfordshire County Record Office reference OxCRO t/SM 6 ii

Flora had been commended for her work in 1886 and 1887, while Edwin was commended in 1889 (not actually receiving the prize as Flora wrote) and her younger sister May was commended in 1894, in the last report to have been preserved.

May Day

The highlight of the children's year was the May Day celebrations which were organised by the school. Several weeks beforehand, the May Queen, usually aged about ten or eleven, was chosen. Making the garland took longer. Instead of the usual crossed hoops of most Oxfordshire garlands, the Cottisford one was pyramid-shaped, based round a light wooden bell shaped about four feet high which required many flowers, bunched and attached closely together, and took a lot of work to decorate. The weekend before the boys would have walked to a wood about six miles away to gather primroses in readiness, and on 30 April the children arrived at school heavily laden with all the flowers they had been able to lay their hands on: cowslips and violets gathered from the fields and wallflowers, oxlips and red flowering currant from their gardens. Greenery was culled from the sweetbriar hedge in the school mistress's garden.

The flowers they had brought invariably proved insufficient and parties of children were despatched to Cottisford House, the Rectory, farms and cottages—anywhere that might produce more flowers for them. Everyone gave generously. Eventually the garland was finished, the top decorated with the coveted crown imperial lilies, and the garland was sprinkled with water and left overnight. The next morning a large china doll in a blue dress was installed sitting on a ledge in the centre of the front of the garland, covered with a white muslin veil, which could be lifted on receipt of payment:

"The attitude of the children to the lady is interesting. It was understood that the garland was her garland, carried in her honour. The lady must never be roughly handled. If the garland turned turtle, as it was apt to do later in the day, when the road was rough and the bearers growing weary, the first question was always, 'Is the lady all right?' (Is it possible that the lady was once 'Our Lady', she having in her turn, perhaps, replaced an earlier effigy of some pagan spirit of the newly decked earth?)"

Lark Rise to Candleford, p.203

The Queen was dressed up in a white frock with a crown of red and white garden daisies, holding her veil in position, while the other girls dressed in white or pale frocks, with veils if possible, both boys and girls being arrayed in bright knots, sashes and bows of ribbon. They were allotted roles, and paraded in order;

"Boy with flag.   Girl with money box.
                THE GARLAND with two bearers.
                        King and Queen.
                      Two maids of honour.
                        Lord and Lady.
                      Two maids of honour.
                   Footman and footman's lady.
                   Rank and file, walking in twos.
Girl known as 'Mother'.   Boy called 'Ragman'."

Lark Rise to Candleford, p. 204

The 'Mother' was a responsible girl who made the children behave well, and carried the lunches in a big basket. The 'Ragman' carried the children's coats, in case of rain. The children first paraded round the village, starting at the Rectory, at about 7 o'clock in the morning, while the Rector was still shaving, where the children would sing the traditional:

"A bunch of May I have brought you
And at your door it stands.
It is but a sprout, but it's well put about
By the Lord Almighty's hands . . ."

Lark Rise to Candleford, p.203

16. May Day was the highlight of the school year for the children. Here the king and queen are shown with the pyramid-shaped garland outside Cotmore House, near Fringford. (Baroness von Maltzahn)

After the Rector's daughter had given them a silver coin, and admired the lady, the children went on to Cottisford House, where more silver would be forthcoming, and a different song sung. They visited all the rest of the houses in the village, carrying on beyond the parish boundary on a seven mile circuit which would have included Shelswell House. It made a long and tiring day for the children, but one they would not have missed for the world, and even when the day was over they could look forward to the money they had collected being shared out the next day at school, and the girls could give the precious doll one last stroke before she was lovingly stored away until the next year.

5

Twyford: Uncle Tom

ໆ໑

Until recently it was believed that the character Flora described in her books as 'Uncle Tom' was the prosperous owner of a shoemaking firm in Market Square in Buckingham by the name of Rechab Holland. However it transpires that 'Uncle Tom' was in fact Thomas Whiting, so when Flora wrote about him and his family being in 'Candleford' she was drawing one of her red herrings over his real home of Twyford, a small village south west of Buckingham, about half way between there and Bicester. Interestingly she is thought to have come to work here herself for a short time at Twyford Post Office when she left Fringford. Twyford is thus part of the 'town' of Candleford, which is a mixture of several different places.

Like Cottisford it was settled before the Norman Conquest but the oldest remaining building is the late twelfth century church of the Assumption of the Blessed Virgin, which has been much altered over the centuries. The Wenman family were lords of the manor in Twyford from 1550 until 1800 when Philip, the last viscount died, after which it passed to a nephew. The Wenmans enclosed Twyford soon after acquiring it. The family moved from Twyford to Oxfordshire in the 18th century and their manor house was turned into a farm, which was demolished in 1857, to be replaced by Twyford Lodge.

With the loss of the Wenman family the village declined in status and by the late 19th century when Flora would have known it was quite small. In 1899 most of the land was owned by Lincoln College, Oxford, Edward James Athawes of Nevill House, Chatham, Owen Clark, a grazier, who lived at Twyford House and Walter Woods of Portway Farm. The population was 349. The Post Office only opened in the mid 1890s, and was listed in Kelly's 1899 Directory of Buckinghamshire:

"Post Office—Miss Elizabeth Cross, sub-postmistress. Letters received from Buckingham at 8.40a.m.; dispatched at 4.40 p.m. week days only. Postal orders are issued here, but not paid. The nearest money order and telegraph office is at Steeple Claydon."

Apart from farming, there were few occupations in the village—two carpenters, three public houses (the Crown, the Red Lion and the Seven Stars), a blacksmith, carrier, haulier, coal merchant, miller, baker and grocer, and butcher and shopkeeper, plus Thomas Whiting, shoe maker.

Thomas Whiting was the son of Austin Masters Whiting, a linen and woollen draper from Roade in Northamptonshire. Austin's career declined, and he was later described as a hawker. Perhaps seeing no future for himself in England he seems to have decided to emigrate, and as his wife did not like the idea, he left her behind. It is not known what happened to him. In the 1861 census Thomas, aged 10, is found in Cottisford living with his grandparents Thomas Batchelor, an agricultural labourer aged 68, born in Buckingham, and his wife Harriet, aged 63 from Blackthorn. Ten years later he was in Juniper Hill, then aged 21 and working as a shoemaker, living with his mother, Mary Whiting, a widow aged 52 who worked as a dressmaker. He was still there in 1876, described in Harrod's *Royal County Directory of Oxfordshire* as a boot and shoemaker of Cottisford (Juniper Hill was not mentioned separately, so he was probably still living there rather than in Cottisford).

He was friendly with Flora's family by 1875, when he and his future wife Ann Timms, Albert's elder sister, were the two witnesses at Emma and Albert Timms' wedding in Cottisford. Their eldest daughter, Mary Martha, was born in Juniper Hill in 1877, but shortly after that they must have moved to Twyford, where he spent the rest of his life, as Ellen Jane was baptised in Twyford on 1 September 1878, Anne Elizabeth on 23 May 1880, Amy on 29 February 1882 and John Austin Whiting on 5 July 1885.

Flora grew to know her uncle and aunt and cousins well, and in *Over to Candleford* recalled her first visit with her parents to visit them. The family got up early in the morning, dressed in their best, and set off in the innkeeper's spring cart. She mentioned going past some earthworks:

"Their father pointed out some earthworks, which, he said, were thrown up by the Romans and described those old warriors in their brass helmets so well that the children seemed to see them; but neither he nor they, dreamed that another field within sight would one day be surrounded by buildings called 'hangars', or that one day, within their own lifetimes, other warriors would soar from it into the sky, armed with more deadly weapons than the Romans ever knew."

Lark Rise to Candleford, pp. 302–3

The earthworks mentioned were probably those known as Fringford Lodge, where Blomfield wrote that an important villa was built on rising ground, to the left of the road:

"When the ground was disturbed here about 1860, two human skeletons were found at a depth of two feet below the surface, the skulls being quite perfect; and several remains of tessellated pavements were laid bare, some tesserae being large and coarse, and others smaller and of different colours, red, blue, and white, the latter probably forming the floor of the hall or other chief room of the house. An underground chamber close by the pavement, with two or three steps leading down to it, was also discovered, which looked as it might have been the site of the hypocaust (warming apparatus) or a bath; and broken pottery abounds. There are also evident signs of an embankment at a short distance in front of this house, over which the present road now runs, and in the adjoining field small coins, mostly copper have been constantly turned up in such numbers as if the ground had been sown broadcast with them."

J.C.Blomfield, *History of the Present Deanery of Bicester*, Part I, 1882

Bicester was once a Roman town called Alchester, so it is not surprising that villas are found in the area. The airfield referred to is R.A.F. Bicester, situated on the Buckingham road, north of the town, which was laid out as a Royal Flying Corps training station in 1916. Several large hangars were built in the 1920s and 30s and bombers were stationed there from 1935.

Flora wrote that Uncle Tom lived in the town of 'Candleford', and it is possible that she knew of Rechab Holland through visiting her grandparents in Buckingham and blended a little of his character with that of Thomas Whiting as the latter was probably not as prosperous as Flora suggests. Flora described her uncle's shop as being the last in the street leaving the town, with one beautiful lady's top boot on a velvet cushion in the shop window, with a sign reading: 'Ladies boots and shoes made to order. Best

Materials. Perfect Workmanship. Fit Guaranteed. Ladies' Hunting Boots a Speciality.'

Most people had their shoes made to measure in those days, so Uncle Tom would have been able to build up a good business in the locality, being the only shoemaker in the village. What is not so certain. however, is that he would have had the workshop Flora describes with workmen and apprentices, although he may have had a small number of employees. Flora grew very fond of her uncle, and sketched his character:

> "If Laura's Uncle Tom was a snob by trade, there was nothing else snobbish about him, for he was one of the most liberal-minded men she was ever to know and one of the wisest. He was a Liberal in politics, too ..."
>
> *Lark Rise to Candleford*, p. 313

Uncle Tom was to have a great influence on Flora. He loved books, and had amassed quite a collection. He was disappointed that his own children did not show much interest in reading, and delighted to help Flora. However, Flora exaggerated when she wrote that he considered them dunces, as they were in fact well educated and well read. When she and Edmund went to stay in Twyford on their own for the first time, aged 11 and 9, Flora discovered a cache of books in the attic. From it she extracted the 18th-century novel *Pamela, or Virtue Rewarded*, by Richardson, which she brought down and devoured eagerly, being dubbed a bookworm by her cousins. Uncle Tom got her to read Mrs Gaskell's *Cranford* to him, and it became a regular thing. Each time she went to stay with her cousins she would sneak into his workshops when she could in the afternoons and read to him while he worked. As she did not have access to such a wealth of books at home, Flora's innate love of books would have been nurtured by her reading with Uncle Tom and being able to borrow some of his books. He was perhaps the first to recognise that she had a special gift, and in consequence encourage her to develop it.

Flora's Aunt Ann was a very slim woman, well educated as she had stayed at school until she was fifteen. She was an affectionate woman, and enormously kind:

> "No one who heard her gentle voice or looked into her fine dark eyes could doubt her loving nature. Her husband laughed at what he called her 'softness' and said that customers calling in a great rage to com-

plain that their shoes had not been delivered to time had stayed to tell the full story of their lives. For her own children she had sweet, pet names, and Edmund was soon her 'little lover' and Laura her 'Pussikins'. Except for her eyes and the dark satiny hair which rippled in waves flat to her head, she was a plain-looking woman, pale and thin of face and of figure so flat that, with her hair parted in the middle and in the long straight frocks she wore, she reminded Laura of Mrs Noah in the toy ark she had given Edmund at Christmas."

Lark Rise to Candleford, p. 313

Ann and Albert's mother, Martha Timms seems to have come to live with the Whitings in her old age, as she was buried at Twyford on 10 August 1886. Flora does not mention having seen her when she came to stay with the family.

Flora's cousins were a little younger than her. Mary Martha, called Molly in the book, was in fact known as Polly, described by Flora as "a motherly little person with a plump, soft figure, red-gold hair, and freckles on the bridge of her nose". (*Lark Rise to Candleford*, p.314). Red hair was not liked in those days, but apparently Rev. H.C.Collier, the vicar of Twyford (this was his real name), admired it. Polly's eldest son, Ernest Arthur, born in 1899, followed in his grandfather's footsteps as bootmaker in Twyford. Her husband Edwin Cherry was a groom at Halton.

Ellen Jane, known as Nellie, was two years younger than Flora who said that she "was dark, quick in her movements, and said things that made people laugh. 'sharp as a needle', said Laura's father afterwards". (*Lark Rise to Candleford*, p.314). She played the piano well.

Both girls were attending a nearby school, and would be sent for a year to 'Miss Bussell's' school to be 'finished'. This could have been Misses Harriet and Louisa Baylis' ladies school in West Street, Buckingham or that of Miss Lydia Mary Roper in Bourton Road, or Miss Anne Warne, St Peter's College. Nellie went on to marry William John Bryan, a railway porter, in 1905.

Anne Elizabeth, (Annie), baptised in 1880, was not as fond of school as her elder sisters, but although she was not so good academically, she excelled at needlework. She later married John Beckett, a labourer from Steeple Claydon in Buckinghamshire, on 25 September 1907 and their son John Austin was baptised in Twyford in 1915.

Amy was the youngest daughter, baptised in 1882, and Flora mentions little about her except that she was good at school work. She never married.

John Austin (Johnny), the last born, in 1885, but the only son, was far more important in the eyes of his parents, and in Flora's eyes, thoroughly spoilt:

> "Johnny must have anything he wanted, no matter to whom it belonged. If Johnny fell down, he must be picked up and comforted . . . He was young for his age and slow in developing; but there was fine stuff in Johnny. As a young man he was deeply religious, a non-smoker, a non-drinker and a non-card player, and served the altar set up on many a battlefield during the 1914–18 War, and all this needed character in the atmosphere of Army life.
>
> That Sunday afternoon Laura saw only a little boy with a pale, freckled face and thin fair hair. A spoilt child, of whom even his parents looked a little ashamed. But, in after years. she also saw Johnny as a sick soldier shut up in Kut, emaciated by illness and hunger and tormented by heat and flies; and that same soldier, once the adored little boy with his bodyguard of sisters, thrown out bodily after an exchange of sick prisoners with a last kick from his native jailer and a 'You can have this one for a makeweight. He's no good.' Or the same Johnny, lying for a whole summer on a long chair in the orchard, fed, every few minutes. as it seemed, with broth, or eggs beaten up in milk, out of teacups, until home and rest and his mother's nursing had strengthened him sufficient to pass his Board and be sent to the trenches in France. For, as we grow older, we see in memory not only our friends as they appeared to us as children, but also as they were to become in later years. "

Lark Rise to Candleford, pp. 314, 317–8

Johnny was in fact considerably younger than Edwin, who was born in 1879. Flora's visits here became some of the highlights of her childhood, with the pleasure in seeing her Uncle Tom who gave her so much encouragement and her affectionate Aunt Ann and her cousins - even spoilt Johnny. She seems to have visited them regularly too while she was working at Fringford, as she wrote that on the Sundays when 'Miss Lane' could spare her she would walk into 'Candleford' for tea with her relatives, enjoying seeing her uncle and aunt, although her cousins were no longer at home. Here she seems to have combined her experiences of working at Fringford and Twyford.

6

Tusmore Park

Tusmore Park situated just down the road from Juniper Hill, must have seemed a remote place to Flora, being the nearest 'great house'. It is unlikely that the family would have had much to do with the aristocracy, but indirectly they had a great influence over the villagers. The aristocracy spent 'the season' in London, but when living at their country houses acted as local magistrates and oversaw the farming of their estates, employing many of the local people. On their shoulders rested the prosperity of the lower classes, so many of whom they employed. On the whole they were respected, but that respect had to be earned, and there was plenty of local gossip about the excesses of the wealthy—gambling away estates, heavy drinking, and the odd orgy!

Tusmore House was a peaceable place, although the village had a fascinating history. The name means *Thurl's Pool* or perhaps, more romantically 'a lake haunted by a giant or demon'. It was one of the villages which had been devastated by the Black Death, being so deserted in 1358 that Sir Roger de Cotesford was able to enclose it and build a house in the park. Nothing of the medieval house is left today. The house that Flora would have known, which replaced the one built for Sir Richard Fermor in 1625, was built from 1766–70 for William Fermor at a cost of £11,305 12s 5½d. The next nine years were spent completing the interior and the gardens. It was designed by Robert Mylne, a Scottish architect, in Italianate style with the principal rooms on the first floor to command better views. Stone for the house came from Fritwell quarry and Headington, with freestone from Glympton and Tottenhoe near Dunstable for features such as columns.

1. Tusmore Park c.1900, showing the exterior built by the Earl of Effingham (John Watts)

2. The saloon at Tusmore Park, described in Kelly's Directory of Berks, Bucks and Oxon 1903 as being the room: "... into which all the rooms open, is panelled in old carved oak, and contains much ancient furniture: on the wall hangs a sketch in oils, by Sir George Hayter, of Her Late Majesty Queen Victoria in Coronation robes: here also are several copies in marble of antiques and a bust of Augustus on a marble pedestal, and here is preserved the saddlecloth of crimson velvet and gold, and the bridle and other trappings of the horse ridden by Kenneth Alexander, Earl of Effingham, as acting Earl Marshal at the coronation of George IV." (John Watts)

The Fermors were a noted Catholic family, several members of whom entered religious orders, and were connected with the prominent Jacobites John and Francis Towneley whose mother was Ursula Fermor. They usually kept a resident priest, often a Jesuit. Mrs Fitzherbert was a frequent guest and according to tradition clandestinely married George IV at Tusmore. However after the death of William Fermor in 1806 the house was let to tenants.

In 1857 the Tusmore Estate was sold so that the proceeds could be divided between the children of the late owner, Captain Ramsay, who had married into the Fermor family. It was described as follows by Messrs Jonas and Thomas Paxton: as being:

"... situated about 5 miles from Bicester, and 4 from Brackley, near to 5 railway stations, and within easy distance of the metropolis; comprising the entire parishes of Tusmore and Hardwick, and portions of the parishes of Stoke Lyne, Fritwell, Cottisford, Souldern, North Aston and Goddington in the county of Oxford, and of Croughton in the county of Northampton, with the capital Mansion of Tusmore, substantially built of stone, erected in 1770 in the Grecian style of architecture, and containing an excellent entrance hall, good breakfast room, spacious dining room 36 feet by 24 and 13 high, a magnificent drawing room 48 feet by 24 and 18 high, a splendid library 36 feet by 24 and 18 high, study, 11 principal bedrooms, 11 secondary apartments, 2 staircases and numerous and suitable offices of the most convenient description, 5 coach houses, capital stabling for 24 horses, gamekeeper's and gardener's cottages, large walled kitchen garden, pleasure grounds, lake, vinery etc. The whole surrounded by a richly timbered park. Adjoining which are several extensive and well stocked game preserves ..."

Quoted in J.C.Blomfield, *History of the Present Deanery of Bicester,* Part III, 1887

Henry Howard, 2nd Earl of Effingham, purchased the estate for £152,000, moving there from The Grange, near Rotherham, where he felt the area was becoming too industrialised, so the rural situation of Tusmore seemed more congenial. He may have known the area previously, as he was educated at Christ Church, Oxford. He came from an eminent family: the first Baron, William Howard, was the first English ambassador to Russia in 1553 and Lord High Admiral of England, while the second baron commanded the English fleet which destroyed the Spanish Armada.

The Earl proceeded to sell some of the outlying estates, but retained 3376 acres. He added an office wing to the main house which spoiled the original symmetry of the design. He changed the main entrance to basement level instead of first-floor level, removing the floor of the original entrance hall to construct a large internal staircase. The library became the new dining room.

The extent of his household and the wide range of servants required to maintain a great house is revealed by the 1871 census. At that time the head of the household, Henry Howard, Earl of Effingham, 64, was in residence with his Canadian wife Eliza, 54, their unmarried daughters Lady Maria, 35, and Lady Alice, 28, and their 4 year old grandson Henry Alexander Gordon Howard.

The principal members of their household staff were Henry Dobson, 41, butler, his wife Elanor, 39, who was the housekeeper, the cook Catherine Roberts, 38, and lady's maids Hannah Dixon, 28, and Mary Dixon, 26. Lower down the scale there were three housemaids: Elizabeth Pudner, 25, Eliza Wadham, 20, and Sarah Williams, 22, plus a kitchen maid, Mary Roberts, 28, scullery maid Maria Mattwood, 21, four laundry maids: Elizabeth Randall, 24, Martha Kirby, 25, Elizabeth Roffe, 17, and Anne Cowley, 16, nursery maid Betsy Fathers, 19, still room maid Ann Giles, 26, and dairy maid Rachel Waters, 27. Other male servants were coachman James Rapple, 35, two footmen: William Poolley, 23, and Edmund Moore, 22, and page George Wickham, 14.

It is interesting to note that the butler and the housekeeper were married to each other, as servants often had to leave their employment when they married. As in most households, there were more female than male servants —16 female to 5 male. Eleanor Dobson, the housekeeper, would have had the task of overseeing the female servants. In the greatest households male cooks were preferred. The ladies' maids would have had higher status than other maids, often coming from the middle rather than lower classes, and had the privilege of travelling with their mistresses. There must have been a lot of washing to justify four laundry maids when there were only three housemaids and one kitchen and one scullery maid. Still Room maids were not common by this time—Ann Giles would probably have been involved in making preserves and perhaps herbal remedies.

Most of Flora's female contemporaries would have gone into service, and many mothers liked their daughters to go onto service in a big house like Tusmore: there was more chance of promotion up the servant ladder than there was working in a farmhouse: "Once a farm-house servant, always a farm-house servant" as they used to say.

TUSMORE.

The Particulars & Conditions of Sale

OF MOST IMPORTANT AND DESIRABLE

FREEHOLD
ESTATES,

COMPRISING THE WHOLE OF THE PARISHES OF

TUSMORE AND HARDWICK,

AND PORTIONS OF THE PARISHES OF

Stoke-Lyne, Fritwell, Cottisford, Souldern, North Aston, and Goddington, in the County of Oxford,

And CROUGHTON in the County of Northampton,

About 5 miles from Bicester, and 4 from Brackley, and within easy reach of 5 Railway stations,

COMPRISING THE

CAPITAL MANSION OF TUSMORE,

With its corresponding Offices and Premises, built of fine Stone, and suitable for the accommodation of a Nobleman or Gentleman's Family,

BEING PLACED IN ITS OWN GROUNDS, WHICH ARE SURROUNDED BY A

RICHLY TIMBERED PARK,

AND WITH

LARGE WALLED GARDEN, VINERY,

Beautiful Lake, Pleasure Grounds, Woods & Plantations.

ALSO SEVERAL

HIGHLY CULTIVATED FARMS,

WITH

EXCELLENT FARM RESIDENCES, AND NUMEROUS COTTAGES,

CONTAINING IN THE WHOLE UPWARDS OF

4700 ACRES,

TOGETHER WITH

The Perpetual Advowsons of the Rectories of Tusmore and Hardwick,

Which will be Sold by Auction,

BY MESSRS.

JONAS & THOS. PAXTON

AT THE AUCTION MART, LONDON,

On Wednesday, the 15th of July, 1857, at 12 o'clock,

By direction of the Trustee under the Will of WILLIAM FERMOR Esquire, deceased.

The Mansion and Estates can be viewed by Ticket only, which with Plans and Particulars can be obtained of Messrs. Tooke, Hallowes and Price, Solicitors, 39 Bedford Row, London; of John M. Davenport, Esq., Clerk of the Peace, Oxford; or of the Auctioneers, Bicester, Oxon. Particulars also at the Queen's Hotel, Manchester; at the Midland Counties Herald Office, Birmingham; or at the Mart.

E. SMITH AND SON, PRINTERS AND STATIONERS, BICESTER.

3. An extract from the sale catalogue of 1857, when Henry Howard, Earl of Effingham, purchased Tusmore Park, indicating the extent of the state. (Centre for Oxfordshire Studies)

The young men working as footmen had probably been chosen for their good physique, as they would open the door to visitors, accompany the family on visits, and thereby reflect credit on their employers. They were seldom selected from among the local boys. Presumably there would have been outdoor male servants living nearby such as gardeners, grooms and coachmen, who did not live in the house,

Although the villagers had little to do with the aristocracy, they noticed when the flag was flying from the tower, indicating that the family were in residence. Flora recalled seeing Henry Howard, Earl of Effingham:

"They sometimes saw him pass through the hamlet in his carriage, an old, old man, sunk deep in cushions and half-buried in rugs, often too comatose to be aware of, or acknowledge, their curtsies. He had never spoken to them or given them anything, for they did not live in his cottages, and in the way of Christmas coals and blankets he had his own parish to attend to; but the men worked on his land, though not directly employed by him, and by some inherited instinct they felt they belonged to him."

Lark Rise to Candleford, pp. 289–90

Lord Effingham was not nearly as old as Flora remembered—he would only have been 69 when she was born. He died in 1889 and was succeeded by his son Henry Howard, 3rd Earl of Effingham (1837–98).

The way of life in such houses was more ritualised than that of the village. The ladies of the house would go out in the carriage to pay calls each afternoon at three o'clock, leaving visiting cards if they found no one in, or else invited friends round to drink tea and play croquet.

The girls who went to work in such houses as servants must have been dumbfounded to see the elaborate decoration and furnishings of these houses compared to the stark furnishings of their own homes. Flora's family were once given a beaded footstool which came from Tusmore House after a fire there, acquired by their landlady 'Mrs Herring', who had no room on the cart for it when she removed the last of her belongings from the 'End House' which Flora's family rented from her:

"But Mrs Herring was back in the closet and, since she could not take all her things away with her, was determined to be generous. 'Now, here's a nice little beaded footstool. Come out of Tusmore House that time the fire was, so you may be sure it's good. You have it, my dear. I'd

4. A group of outdoor servants in the courtyard at Tusmore Park, showing, from left to right: Joseph Walby, the gamekeeper, Mr. Rouse, a footman, Jack Allen (brother of Richard Allen, who later served as land agent to the Earl of Effingham), with a jug of beer, and another footman and a groom. (John Watts, characters identified by G. Allen)

like you to have it'. Their mother eyed the little round stool with the claw legs and beaded cover. She would really have liked that, but had made up her mind to accept nothing. Perhaps, she reflected, too, that it would be hers in any case, as what Mrs Herring could not take she would have to leave, for she said again: 'It's very kind of you, I'm sure, but I don't know that I've any use for it.' "

Lark Rise to Candleford, p.296

There are few direct references to Tusmore in *Lark Rise to Candleford*, and Flora is unlikely ever to have set foot inside it, but she was delighted to discover after her book was published that Lady Bicester, wife of the then owner of Tusmore Park, liked it, and commented to her sister ". . . such praise makes me feel very humble. It is rather amusing to think of my books being read at Tusmore. Father helped to finish rebuilding that house." (Quoted from a letter published in the *Bicester Advertiser*, 20 May 1973).

The house Flora knew was demolished in 1960 and a new house built, itself now destroyed, although some of the old farm buildings, including a half-timbered dovecote on staddle stones, still remain.

7

Shelswell

෧

Shelswell Park was the second 'great house' which featured in Flora's life. It is situated between Cottisford and Fringford, and her first experience of the house must have been as one of the group of Cottisford schoolchildren carrying their may garland both here and to Tusmore each year:

1. A detail of Shelswell House, built in 1875 and demolished in the 1980s, illustrating the crest of the Slater Harrison family. (Bodleian Library)

"It was at the back door of large houses that the fun began. In country houses at that date troops of servants were kept, and the May Day procession would find the courtyard crowded with house-maids and kitchen-maids, dairy-maids and laundry-maids, footmen, grooms, coachmen, and gardeners. The songs were sung, the garland was admired; then to a chorus of laughter, teasing and urging, one Maid of Honour snatched the cap from the King's head, the other raised the Queen's veil, and a shy, sheepish boy pecked at his companion's rosy cheek, to the huge delight of the beholders.

'Again! Again!' a dozen voices would cry and the kissing was repeated until the royal couple turned sulky and refused to kiss any more, even when offered a penny a kiss. Then the lord saluted his lady and the footman the footman's lady (this couple had probably been introduced in compliment to such patrons), and the money-box was handed round and began to grow heavy with pence.

The menservants, with their respectable side-whiskers, the maids in their little flat caps like crocheted mats on their smoothly parted hair, and their long, billowing lilac or pink print gowns, and the children in their ribbon-decked poverty, alike belonged to a bygone order of things. The boys pulled forelocks and the girls dropped curtseys to the upper servants, for they came next in importance to 'the gentry'...

After the mansion, there were the steward's, the head gardener's and the stud-groom's houses to visit with the garland; then on through the gardens and park and woods and fields to the next stopping-place."

Lark Rise to Candleford, p. 208

There was no real village of Shelswell in the nineteenth century, only a few houses near the house, lived in by important employees such as the gardener, gamekeeper, blacksmith and the two farmers, William Ladler and Thomas Badam, who leased their farms from the Harrisons who owned Shelswell. The area was probably settled in Saxon times, as the place-name means the spring or stream of Scield, an Anglo-Saxon personal name. Only traces of moats indicate the site of the medieval manor house near Home Farm, with the site of St Ebbe's church (it was not used after the 17th century and was demolished by 1796) and the deserted medieval village nearby. Like Tusmore, the land was enclosed early, here in 1601. In the early 18th century the Trotman family built a new manor house.

Gilbert Harrison, a London merchant, purchased the estate in the 18th

2. All that remains of Shelswell House is the stable block.

century, and was succeeded by his son John who died in 1834. The house then descended to John's nephew, another John, son of his sister Ann Harrison and John Slater of Margate, on condition that he use the surname Harrison, so he complied by changing his name to John Slater-Harrison. He married Louisa, daughter of the second Earl of Clonmell, grand-daughter of the second Earl of Warwick, who died in 1873 aged 66. John Slater-Harrison died the following year in 1874, aged 70, and was succeeded by his son Edward Slater-Harrison, the 'Sir Timothy' of *Lark Rise to Candleford* who was born at Shelswell. He played an important role in county affairs, acting as High Sheriff in 1882, as a Justice of the Peace on the Bicester Bench, and an elected member of the first Oxfordshire County Council in 1888. He was also Colonel of the Bicester corps of the Oxfordshire Yeomanry Cavalry.

The 1881 census indicates the composition of his household, which was much smaller than that of the Earl of Effingham: Edward Slater Harrison, head, aged 48, Magistrate and Captain of Yeomanry, was in residence with his wife Cecilia, aged 48. Their staff consisted of butler Oliver Damp, 54, housekeeper Maria Holfman, 35, German lady's maid Maren Wiegand, 27, housemaids Ellen Kay, 41 and Sophie Savin, 22, kitchen maid Emily Cook, 24, scullery maid Mary Fensmore, aged 20, footman Charles Hadland, 24, and under footman Charles Ansford, 17.

The house that Flora would have known was very modern, having been built for Edward Slater-Harrison in 1875. He demolished most of the eighteenth century house and commissioned architect William Wilkinson, famous for his many North Oxford houses, to design his new one, Italianate in style, in Bath stone, which was embellished with the Slater and Harrison family crests and a datestone reading 1875. Part of the eighteenth century house was incorporated into the new building, housing the billiard room. (This house in its turn has been demolished, and all that is left is the stable block). Slater-Harrison enlarged Shelswell Park and made several plantations, increasing the size of the gardens and laying out new ornamental gardens north of the house. Blomfield, who knew him, evidently considered him to be a good influence on the area, as he wrote in his *History of the Present Deanery of Bicester*, pp. 17–18:

> "These houses of the squirearchy, who are in residence on their estates the greater part of the year, are elements of considerable blessing to the country. Their families are always in the midst of the people, knowing and attentive to the history, wants and infirmities of everyone. The ladies look after the sick, the schools, the young girls at home and those gone to service; the squire takes an interest in the general good of the parish and district; holds important offices connected with their management. Money is freely spent on the estate, and a considerable amount of culture and moral restraint is acquired in the classes below, in the farmhouses and the cottages. Those persons only who have known parishes that have been for generations squireless, and also those where a good squire and his family have been settled for a similar time, can appreciate the difference in general tones among the people."

It was to Shelswell Park that Flora and her family went for the celebrations in honour of Queen Victoria's Jubilee in 1887. Having been almost forgotten for years, Queen Victoria suddenly became a popular figure, her name on everybody's lips; people were proud to contribute a penny each, collected by Miss Sawkins Harrison, the Vicar's daughter, to buy their Queen a present, and, most exciting of all, a big celebration for the villagers from nearby parishes took place at Shelswell Park.

At midday on the day of the Jubilee the family at the End House began their preparations for the great day: the children and their mother were washed and brushed and put in their best clothes, and only given a snack lunch so that they would not spoil their appetite for the treat. Flora's father refused to come on principle and went to work instead, so Emma, accompanied by Flora, aged 10, Edwin, aged 8, and 3 year old May with new-born baby Elizabeth in the baby carriage, walked to Shelswell.

3. A group of people dressed in their best, thought to be on their way to celebrate Queen Victoria's Golden Jubilee in 1887 in Shelswell Park. (John Watts)

4. A marquee erected in Banbury with food laid out to celebrate Queen Victoria's jubilee in 1897. A similar one was set up in Shelswell Park in 1887. (Oxfordshire Photographic Archive)

It must have been quite daunting to see the milling crowds on their arrival in the Park—in the ordinary course of events they would not see many people, so they must have had feelings both of excitement and fear. As well as the expected feast, they were greeted by the sight of a small fair in progress, with roundabouts, swings and coconut shies, and music from hurdy-gurdys and a brass band.

To control the numbers, each parish in turn was invited into the marquee for their tea—after the meagre fare at home the quantity of food must have been almost unbelievable—clothes baskets filled with slices of bread spread with butter and jam and dough cakes washed down with tea from watering cans. There was so much there that few could resist slipping some food into their pockets to take home after they had eaten their fill.

After tea there were the usual sports and entertainments: races and high jump competitions, sideshows such as dipping heads into water tubs to bring up sixpences with the teeth, and traditional country games such as grinning through a horse collar—in other words the winner was the one who could make the most hideous face—and the one the housewives hated, because it ruined trousers—climbing the greasy pole to take the leg of mutton (almost roasted in the sunshine) from the top.

The celebrations ended with fireworks as it grew dark, but what fascinated Flora most was the tight-rope dancing, and for ages afterwards she delighted in pirouetting along five-barred gates.

When she visited Shelswell Park for the jubilee celebrations she could have had no idea that only four years later she would be going into the house and meeting the owner! When she went to work for Mrs Whitton at Fringford Forge at the age of fourteen, before she was permitted to so much as handle a letter in the post office she had to be sworn in before a Justice of the Peace—in this case Edward Slater-Harrison at Shelswell:

"The interview next morning did not turn out so terrifying as Laura had expected. Sir Timothy smiled very kindly upon her when the

5. Edward Slater Harrison, owner of Shelswell Park, the magistrate to whom Flora had to swear official oaths of loyalty to the Post Office when she first went to work at Fringford Post Office. (Baroness von Maltzahn)

footman ushered her into his Justice Room, saying: 'The young person from the Post Office, please, Sir Timothy.'

'What have you been up to? Poaching, rick-burning, or petty larceny?' he asked when the footman had gone. 'If you're as innocent as you look, I shan't give you a long sentence, So come along,' and he drew her by the elbow to the side of his chair. Laura smiled dutifully, for she knew by the twinkle of his keen blue eyes beneath their shaggy white eyebrows that Sir Timothy was joking.

As she leaned forwards to take up a pen with which to sign the thick blue official document he was unfolding, she sensed the atmosphere of jollity, good sense, and good nature, together with the smell of tobacco, stables, and country tweeds he carried around, like an aura.

'But read it! Read!' he cried in a shocked voice, 'Never put your name to anything before you have read it or you'll be signing your own death warrant one of these days.' And Laura read out, as clearly as her shyness permitted, the Declaration which even the most humble candidate for Her Majesty's Service had in those serious days to sign before a magistrate.

'I do solemnly promise and declare that I will not open or delay or cause or suffer to be opened or delayed any letter or anything sent by the post', it began, and went on to promise secrecy in all things.

When she had read it through, she signed her name, Sir Timothy signed his, then folded the document neatly for her to carry back to Miss Lane, who would send it on to the higher authorities."

Lark Rise to Candleford, pp. 402–3

For a few months in her career at the post office she acted as letter carrier, so frequently visited Shelswell Park with 'Sir Timothy's' post in a locked private postbag. The footmen, who resented the fact that their private mail was also locked in the bag, gave Flora a hard time, teasing her unmercifully, but she did not dare complain to Mrs Whitton.

It was while she was walking in the grounds in the course of her duties that she had an interesting encounter, which could have changed the future course of her life, with a young gamekeeper, armed with a shotgun, who accused her of trespassing. Flora christened him 'Philip White' in *Candleford Green*:

"He was a tall, well-built young man, apparently in the middle twenties, with a small fair moustache and very pale blue eyes which, against

6. A gamekeeper with a shooting party and beaters, possibly from Shelswell Park.
(John Watts)

his dark tanned complexion, looked paler. His features might have
been called handsome but for their set rigidity."

Lark Rise to Candleford, p.518

They got chatting once he realised that she was no threat to his precious
pheasants, and he told her all about his family, including his gamekeeper
father and his sister who worked in a draper's shop in Oxford. After that he
contrived to meet her in the course of her journeys through the park most
days, and even kissed her shyly when they went through the kissing gate.
He was her first boyfriend, and she supposed they counted as sweethearts,
daydreaming that as his wife she could help him feed the pheasant chicks
and live in a little cottage. However the thought of Philip being there too
brought her down to earth; she was not truly in love with him, and was old
enough to realise that he was a selfish and self-centred man. Much to her
surprise and embarrassment he turned up to see her at the post office one
evening, and talked to her within Mrs Whitton's hearing, demanding that
she take a few days off to come and visit his mother. This was tantamount to
a proposal of marriage and Flora was dumbfounded, terrified of what Mrs
Whitton would think. Philip continued "You are my girl, aren't you,
Laura?" to which Flora responded rather desperately: "You've never asked
me." At this Philip took her hand and said: "Well, I thought you understood. But don't be frightened. You will be my girl, won't you, Laura?"
Flora commented rather sadly:

> "That was inadequate enough as a declaration of love, but Laura's
> answer was even more inadequate. 'No—no thank you, Philip,' she
> said, and the most unromantic love scene on record was over, for,
> without another word, he turned, went out of the door and out of her
> life. She never saw him again to speak to."

Lark Rise to Candleford, pp. 521–2

To her great relief, Mrs Whitton was not censorious or reproachful of her
behaviour and little was made of the incident.

While she was working in Fringford she encountered Cecilia Slater-
Harrison, Sir Edward's second wife, the greatest lady in her immediate
area, to whom she gave the name of 'Lady Adelaide':

> "For Lady Adelaide, Sir Timothy's wife, the footman usually did busi-
> ness while she sat in her carriage outside, but occasionally she herself

would come rustling in, bringing with her a whiff of perfume, and sink languidly down in the chair provided for customers on their side of the counter. She was a graceful woman, and it was a delight to watch her movements . . . She was tall and thin and, Laura thought, aristocratic-looking."

Lark Rise to Candleford, p. 465

Flora was embarrassed when Lady Cecilia spoke to her and invited her to join the Conservative Primrose League, of which she was local patron, because her parents were Liberals and would greatly disapprove of her doing so, she plucked up all her courage to decline politely. She only realised afterwards that her Ladyship had done her a kindness. Her father had imbued her with his independence of spirit, which shone through her shyness and gave her the strength and perseverance to work hard to achieve her aims in life, particularly in her writing.

1. 1879 Ordnance Survey map of Fringford. Flora lived with Mrs Whitton in the building marked 'Smithy'. (Centre for Oxfordshire Studies)

8

Fringford: Candleford Green

ॐ

When Flora left *Lark Rise* behind, and began to write about 'Candleford' and 'Candleford Green', she openly admitted that she took a lot more liberties with her material, and deliberately combined several places into one. It was to 'Candleford Green' that she went to work in the Post Office for 'Miss Lane' at the age of fourteen in 1891, living away from home for the first time, and enjoying her first taste of independence.

'Candleford Green' is partly based on Flora's knowledge of Fringford, with elements drawn from her work in other Post Offices in different parts of the country, but many of the physical characteristics of Fringford are nothing like those of 'Candleford Green'. She depicted her 'Candleford Green' as a suburb of the town of Candleford, whereas in reality it is a medium-sized village, well away from the nearest town of Bicester, so her descriptions have to be treated with circumspection. However Fringford, like 'Candleford Green', is a much larger and more varied village than either Juniper Hill or Cottisford, so Flora was able to widen her experience of life. It was described in the 1880s by Blomfield:

> "This village, as it now appears, is prettily situated on the slope of a gentle eminence northwards. It is a quiet spot, remote from public traffic, there being no highway through it. The only approach to it is from the west. Three roads (a branch from the Buckingham and Bicester road, a road from Stoke and Caversfield, and a third descending from Hethe) meet close to one point, where is the only access to this village. This opens on the Green, and then divides into two roads,

2. Fringford village green, looking south, *c.*1910 (William Plumb)

which cross it in different directions. On two sides of the Green are some old, picturesque houses, and in a hollow at its north end is a large pound, near which may generally be seen a few representatives of the geese tribe, who through many long years have fed and quacked upon the greensward. Here, too, stands the Schoolroom, unenclosed. The road, passing these, leads on to some of the cottages, and beyond them to the Rectory-house. The church is not visible from the Green, but the second road, running eastward, leads to it, and to the present Manor-house, and some other houses of the villagers. There is no street here, as in most other villages, the various buildings lying scattered apart from each other."

D. C. Blomfield, *History of the Present Deanery of Bicester*, Part V, 1890/91

A notable family was the Addingtons who moved to the village in the 16th century; in 1597 William and Henry Addington, a yeoman and husbandman, bought 2000 year leases to two and a half yardlands from the manor. Henry Addington held the important posts of constable and churchwarden in 1662 and 1664, and it was his son William who was the first of the family to call himself a gentleman and aspire to a family pew in the church.

His son, Dr. Anthony Addington (1713–90), was William Pitt's doctor. He and his wife Mary, who died in 1778, are commemorated in the church by a monument which was designed by Richard Westmacott, and shows the arms of the Addington family. Addington and the rector started a school in the village in 1768, and his family continued to support it. The house he lived in on the green, which is now incorporated into Hall Farm, near the forge, is basically 16th century although it has been much altered over the years. Flora described it as a "tall old red-brick Georgian farmhouse, where judging by its size and appearance, people of importance must once have lived, but where then only an old cowman and his wife occupied one corner." (*Lark Rise to Candleford*, p. 418). Addington's son Henry was Prime Minister from 1801–4 and was created Lord Sidmouth.

Many different families held the manor over the next few centuries, until in 1815 it was purchased by John Harrison of Shelswell Park. The land had already been enclosed in 1762, which increased its value and the population increased from 252 in 1801 to 479 in 1871. In 1901 there were 94 dwellings. The village grew up round a large green, with the church and manor house to the north, where the village pound was situated.

As at Juniper Hill and Cottisford the principal occupation in Fringford was farming, although Fringford boasted a much wider range of employment. The main farms were Manor, Glebe and Waterloo Farm, (the house there was built by John Harrison and named after Wellington's victory over Napoleon), and the outlying Cotmore Farm which has the remains of a medieval moat. In 1891 there were fifty-four agricultural labourers, one cowman, five shepherds (one retired), five carters, one plough boy and one field woman, plus one farm bailiff and three farmers, (Henry King of Waterloo Farm, John Simons at the Manor House and George Gibbard who was also a maltster and brewer, who employed one assistant). Connected with farming were two agricultural machinists, a woodman and a hurdle-maker.

In addition to those involved in farming, several people worked as servants, including four housekeepers, twelve domestic servants, three farm servants, one housemaid, one laundry maid, two footmen, two coachmen, two grooms and six gardeners. Other occupations included a carrier and two assistants, a coal haulier, shoemaker, Army Reserve, timber carrier, two brickmakers and one assistant, bricklayer, stonemason, painter, plumber and decorator, decorator, four blacksmiths (one also postmaster), three carpenters, two wheelwrights, five general labourers, butcher, baker, grocer, one licensed victualler (Richard Hood at the Butcher's Arms), timber carter and interestingly two lawyers. Three lived on their own means, and there was a midwife, a charwoman, two laundresses and a letter carrier. The range is far bigger than that of Cottisford. Flora appreciated this and commented of Fringford:

> "In the hamlet there lived only one class of people; all did similar work, all were poor and all were equal ... The village was a little world in itself; the hamlet was but a segment."
>
> *Lark Rise to Candleford*, p. 416

Flora must have been fascinated by the variety of shops in the village, having been used to only a tiny store in the back room of the pub. According to the 1891 census there were a butcher, a baker and a grocer in Fringford, who may well have been situated together on the Green, but not the Stores described by Flora, owned by Ruby and Pearl, which sold smart clothes, which she must have seen in a town and transposed. Flora described Tarman's the grocers (if she was referring to the real one in Fringford, it was run by Mark Mansfield) and the butcher's, (run by John Clarke), who fulfilled an important role in village life:

> "... the grocer catered for all. At that time the more important village people, such as the doctor and clergyman, bought their provisions at the village shop as a matter of principle ... and even the rich who spent only part of the year at their country houses or their hunting boxes believed it their duty to give the local tradesman a turn. If there happened to be more businesses than one of a kind in a village, orders were placed with each alternately ...
>
> A grocer had to be a grocer then, for his goods did not come to him in packets, ready to be handed over the counter, but had to be selected and blended and weighed out by himself, and for quality he was directly responsible to his customers. The butcher, too, received no stiff, shrouded carcasses by rail, but had to be able to recognize the points in the living animal at the local market sufficiently quickly and well to be able to guarantee the succulent joints and the old-fashioned chops and steaks would melt in the mouth. Even his scrag ends of mutton and sixpen'orth of pieces of beef which he sold to the poor were tasty and rich with juices which the refrigerator seems to have destroyed in present-day meat."
>
> *Lark Rise to Candleford*, pp. 462-3

The National school, built in 1866 by Henry de Salis, then rector, was on the far side of the village green from the Post Office. It was a typical village school, big enough to justify two teachers, the average attendance in 1871 being 73. The building is no longer used for the school, which now occupies a modern building on the other side of the green.

South west of the village on the road to Bicester are Cotmore House, built in 1857 by William Dewar and his wife Augusta (née Slater-Harrison), and Fringford Lodge, built in 1814 by Rev. Herbert John Beaver, and enlarged by Rev. E. Withington in the 1870s, in the grounds of which are the remains of a Roman villa, mentioned by Flora's father Albert as they drove past it on the journey to 'Candleford'.

The Church

The church, dedicated to St Michael and All Angels, is tucked away at the bottom of the village. There was a church here at least as early as 1103, and the earliest remaining portion, the restored south door and two arches in the nave, date from the twelfth century, and some delightful carved heads feature on the thirteenth-century south piers. Much of what one can see today only dates from the 19th century when substantial repairs were made to the church which had been allowed to decay by many non-resident lords of the manor.

The Rectory, approached by a footpath from the church, is a large, mainly nineteenth-century house, incorporating a much earlier kitchen wing. The Rector when Flora arrived was Cadwallader Coker, a wealthy man, aged 66 in 1891, who came from Bicester House, Bicester, and had been there since 1874, living with his wife Emily, aged 69 from Ilfracombe, their spinster daughters Marianne and Emily, aged 39 and 35 and three domestic servants. Flora would have attended church regularly with Mrs Whitton and gave her usual cogent description of Rev. Coker and his wife:

"He was an elderly man with what was then known as a fine presence, being tall and large rather than stout, with rosy cheeks, a lion-like mane of white hair, and an air of conscious authority. His wife was a dumpy little roly-poly of a woman who wore old, comfortable clothes about the village because, as she was once heard to say, 'Everybody here knows who I am, so why bother about dress?' For church and for afternoon calls upon her equals, she dressed in the silks and satins and ostrich feathers befitting her rank as the granddaughter of an earl and the wife of a vicar with large private means. She was said by the villagers to be 'a bit managing', but, on the whole, she was popular with them."

Flora Thompson, Lark Rise to Candleford, p. 424

Flora wrote that Mrs Coker contracted a fatal illness at a summer bazaar, which rapidly killed both her and her husband. They did indeed die within a few days of each other, but in the spring—Emily Coker on 14 April aged 71 and her husband on the 23 April 1894, aged 69. His successor was Rev. C.G. Thompson, rechristened Rev. Delafield by Flora, a very different character: a young man in his early thirties, who apparently always looked untidy, he was

> "somewhat inclined to premature bulkiness, whose large, pink, clean-shaven face had a babyish look, which his fair hair, worn rather long and inclined to curl, did nothing to dispel. Dignity did not enter into his composition."

Lark Rise to Candleford, p. 523

The Delafields did not have the private means of their predecessors, but Mrs Delafield was notable for wearing Bohemian clothes—long loose dresses very different in style from the corseted clothes worn by most of her contemporaries.

Post Office and Forge

The Post Office where Flora was to live occupied a prominent position near the Green:

> "Miss Lane's house was a long, low white one, with the Post Office at one end and a blacksmith's forge at the other. On the turf in front of the door was a circular iron platform with a hole in the middle which was used for putting on tyres to wagon and cart wheels, for she was a wheelwright as well as blacksmith and postmistress. She did not work in the forge herself; she dressed in silks of which the colours were brighter than those usually worn by women of her age and had tiny white hands which she seldom soiled. Hers was the brains of the busi-

3. The Post Office and forge, Fringford, before 1891. John Whitton, the post-master and blacksmith, stands in front of the spring cart with his wife Kezia, (Flora's 'Miss Lane') who holds the horse's head. Zilpha Hinks, at that time their servant, stands in the doorway. The little girl cannot be identified. The man with the sledgehammer on the left is William Elderfield, the man next to him is unidentified, and the third is Frederick William Plumb, (Flora's 'Matthew' the foreman). The square of metal on the grass in front of the forge is the tyreing platform. (William Plumb)

ness . . . She was then about fifty, a little birdlike woman in her kingfisher silk dress, with snapping black eyes, a longish nose, and black hair plaited into a crown on top of her head."

Lark Rise to Candleford, pp. 362–3

Flora added that there was a scarlet-painted letter box let into the wall and a signboard reading "*Candleford Green Post and Telegraph Office*", with another one above the forge reading "*Dorcas Lane, Shoeing and General Smith*". This cannot have been entirely accurate, as at that time, contrary to what Flora wrote, there was no telegraph machine in Fringford, and John Whitton would probably still have been in charge when she first arrived, although he was very ill, dying on 28 August 1891 aged 61.

Kezia Whitton, who was baptised in Stoke Lyne on 11 January 1835, was the youngest of three daughters of Elizabeth and Alexander Kirby, the village blacksmith, who was buried in Stoke Lyne in 1864. Elizabeth died aged 75 in 1873. Alexander does not appear ever to have been the blacksmith in Fringford, but in 1851 another Kirby was in charge there, who may have been a relative. The 1851 census tells us that in Fringford John Kirby, aged 78 from Fritwell, lived at the forge with his son John, aged 49, born in Croughton, and his grandsons Thomas aged 19, John aged 17 and William aged 11, who were all blacksmiths born in Fringford, and his 9 year old grand-daughter Elizabeth. It is not known what happened to the Kirbys after 1851, but by 1854 John Whitton was at 24 running the forge, so Kezia probably came to Fringford with him.

Kezia Whitton was, like her husband, but unlike 'Miss Lane' very large, weighing over eighteen stone, although Flora later wrote that the mental attributes she gave to Miss Lane were all those of Kezia Whitton. The Whittons had three children, Annie Louisa, who died as an infant in 1860, George, born in 1863, and Alexander born in 1866. Alexander died at the age of 24 in Africa, when working as accountant on the Gold Coast. George elected not to become a blacksmith, becoming a Customs and Excise Officer in Liverpool instead.

It was most unusual at that time for a woman to choose to carry on her husband's business, let alone something like a smithy, but Kezia had no hesitation. She had a strong personality which fitted her for an important role in village life, and Flora commented that in another era she would probably have made much more of a mark in the world. She enjoyed the Post Office, because this gave her the opportunity to find out legitimately all about the village affairs, and as both the smithy and the Post Office were

4. John Whitton (1830–1891) and his wife Kezia (1835–98) with their sons Alexander Kirby Whitton (1866–89), local auditor of the Gold Coast Company and George Whitton (born 1863), a Customs and Excise Officer in Liverpool. Behind them stands their blacksmith foreman Frederick William Plumb (1859–1930). (William Plumb)

central to village life. Her work gave her a position of authority locally. She was an organised person, and her Post Office reflected this, with all the forms neatly arranged in pigeon holes. The Post Office counter was fixed across the through passage of the house, and could be folded down against the wall with wooden shutters constructed so as to close it off.

Flora came to the job with no experience, only an aptitude for figures. She would have found it difficult, if not impossible, to have obtained a job in a bigger town post office as women of higher birth were preferred, and the Post Office expected female employees to pass Civil Service exams, which Flora did not have the basic education to be able to take. However, the experience she acquired in Fringford enabled her to work in other Post Offices including her husband's during the war.

When she first arrived in the post office she was petrified—at her first tea there she was offered a Banbury cake, a great luxury at home, but was too nervous to eat it! She realised that she had many things to learn:

"Even in that small country Post Office there was in use what seemed to her a bewildering number and variety of official forms, to all of which Miss Lane who loved to make a mystery of her work referred by a number, not name, But soon, in actual practice, 'AB/35', 'K.21', 'X.Y.13', or what not became 'The blue Savings Bank Form', 'The Postal Order Abstract', 'The Cash Account Sheet' and so on, and Laura found herself flicking them out of their pigeon-holes and carrying them without a moment's hesitation to where Miss Lane sat doing her accounts at the kitchen table.

Then the stamps! The 1d. and ½d. ones she already knew by sight were in 10s. and 5s. sheets which hot, nervous hands were inclined to tear, and those of higher value, neatly hinged in a cardboard-leaved book, ready to be sold for parcels and telegrams, had to be detached just so, working up from the left-hand bottom corner. And the cash drawer, with its three wooden bowls for gold, silver, and copper, and all three bowls at least half-full, even the one for sovereigns and half-sovereigns! What a lot of money there must be in the world! Laura would

5. Mr Hornsby, the postman to Hethe, Fringford, Stratton Audley and Stoke Lyne, *c.*1900. (John Watts)

run her fingers through the shining gold coins when the cash was counted at night and placed in the black japanned box ready to be taken upstairs, wrapped in an old woolly shawl as disguise, and stood on the top shelf of Miss Lane's clothes cupboard. Occasionally there was a banknote in the japanned box, but no Treasury notes, for there were none issued."

Lark Rise to Candleford, pp. 404–5

In those days notes were issued by small local banks not by the Bank of England. The morning mail was brought on foot from Bicester at 7a.m.. The postman in 1891, according to Pankhurst's Almanack and Directory, was Postman Plater, whose round included Hethe, Fringford, Newton Morrell, Willaston and Shelswell. Flora opened up his sack in what had once been a wash-house, which had sorting benches arranged around it. The postman waited while the village mail was sorted out for him to take and female letter carriers were employed for outlying places. Flora called the morning postman Thomas Brown,

" a stockily built man with greying hair, who had, as far as was known always led a quiet, respectable life. Until recently he had taken great interest in local affairs and had such good judgement that he had occasionally been asked to arbitrate in local disputes."

Lark Rise to Candleford, p. 407

He had been converted to Methodism, which altered his outlook on life. According to the Almanack another postman, Hudson, delivered mid-day to Stratton Audley, Fringford, Hethe and Stoke Lyne.

Flora caught the eye of Walter Joseph French, the postmaster in the main Post Office in Bicester Market Place, whom she christened Mr Rushton. He came to visit the Fringford Post Office twice a year to ensure that the business was being conducted properly. All the account books, cash and papers were neatly laid out for him on the kitchen table ready to be checked:

"It was an old-fashioned way of conducting business and Mr Rushton was an old-fashioned postmaster. He was a neat, middle-aged little man, very precise in his speech and manner, and with what many considered an exaggerated sense of his own importance. Pleasant, if somewhat patronizing to well-doers on his staff, but a terror to the careless and slipshod worker. He was under the impression that his own office staff adored him. 'The crew of my little ship know who is captain.' It is sad to have to record that the crew in private spoke of their captain as 'Holy Joe'."

Lark Rise to Candleford, p. 410

This last reference is to the fact that he was a Methodist, and wore black or dark grey clothes. He spotted Flora's potential and had hoped to be able to offer her promotion to Bicester Post Office, but neither of his female clerks, who were in fact Miss Wrapson and Miss Toovey, married, so no vacancy arose for Flora. Perhaps it was frustration at not being able to find a better job locally that made her decide that it was time to see a little of the world when she left Fringford.

Flora did not, as she wrote, see a telegraph machine on her visit to the forge as a child, but one was installed during her time at the Post Office, and her skill at working it stood her in good stead in later life. The telegraph machine was carefully housed in the front room, given an air of domesticity by being hidden under a cover similar to a tea cosy:

"The telegraph machine had been installed in the parlour, where its scientific-looking white dials and brass trimmings looked strikingly modern against Miss Lane's old rosewood and mahogany furniture. It was what was known as the ABC type of instrument . . . it served very well in its day, being easy to learn and reliable in working . . . The ABC was read by sight. A handle, like that of a coffee mill, guided a pointer from letter to letter on a dial which had the alphabet printed round it, clockwise, and this came out and was read on a smaller dial at the other end of the circuit. Surrounding the operating dial were brass studs or keys, one for each letter, and the operator, turning the handle with one hand, depressed the keys with the finger of the other, and by doing so spelt out the words of a telegram. A smaller dial above, known as the 'receiver', recorded incoming messages."

Lark Rise to Candleford, p. 412

Flora described two letter carriers, but only one was listed in the 1891 census, and surprisingly that one was Zilpha Hinks, who must be the person Flora described as Zillah, Kezia Whitton's crusty rheumatic servant. Zilpha appeared, aged 16, as a pupil teacher in the 1871 census, the daughter of an agricultural labourer. In 1881 she was indeed living with the Whittons, aged 26, as a general servant, but by 1891 she was back at home with her widowed mother, four grown up sisters who worked as servants and two brothers who were agricultural labourers. Flora described her as old and flat-footed, with a bit of a temper and a shrill laugh and said that her darning was so crude that it could be seen across the room. She tolerated Flora's presence and was glad of her help running errands around the house, but she always treated her with a measure of suspicion. There is obviously a good deal of artistic license in this depiction of Zillah, who would only have been thirty-six when Flora came to the forge. As she had been intelligent enough to be a pupil teacher, perhaps she would have liked to have had Flora's job rather than that of letter carrier. It is ironic that she became a letter carrier in real life because Flora wrote about an incident when 'Mrs Macey', the letter carrier, had to go off and see her husband who was dangerously ill in Dartmoor prison, leaving 'Miss Lane' with a dilemma:

> "The thing now is what we are going to do about the letters and Sir Timothy's private postbag. Zillah shan't go. I wouldn't demean myself to ask her, after the disgraceful way she's been banging away upstairs, not to mention her bad feet and her rheumatism."
>
> *Lark Rise to Candleford*, p. 505

The upshot of that exchange was that Flora, to her delight, became a letter carrier. This gave her a chance to wander the countryside and extend her knowledge of natural history, which proved a deep interest throughout her life. Zilpha Hinks was certainly not the old woman of *Candleford Green*, as she died in January 1900 aged only 45. Mrs Whitton's servant in the 1891 census was Winifred Waring, a girl of only 14, who was termed 'general servant'—again nothing like the old woman described in the book.

Flora enjoyed the new freedom and independence she found working at the Post Office. She must have delighted in the access she had to Mrs Whitton's books, which she eagerly read at every spare moment. She even found time to do a little writing of her own, which she later destroyed in Grayshott when she met 'real' writers, and felt how inadequate her own attempts had been.

She noted how Kezia Whitton ran her household on the same strict old-fashioned lines as she ran the Post Office. This presented Flora with a problem: Kezia followed the traditional method of having a washerwoman in to do her washing every six weeks, and poor Flora did not have enough clothes to last that long, so she had to parcel up her dirty washing and send

6. The forge, Fringford, *c*.1898. Frederick William Plumb is sitting in the cart and the boys may be Mrs Whitton's grandsons. (William Plumb)

it home to her mother each week via two different carriers' carts. However it was a treat to get the parcel of clean clothes back with a little present of cakes, home made food or flowers from her mother, and it gave her a link with home.

Kezia's traditional attitude was wonderfully exemplified by her style at table:

> "At the head of the long, solid oak table sat 'the mistress', with an immense dish of meat before her, carving knife in hand. Then came a reserved space, sometimes occupied by visitors, but more often blank table-cloth; then Matthew's chair, and, after that, another, smaller blank space, just sufficient to mark the difference in degree between a foreman and ordinary workmen. Beyond that, the three young men sat

in a row at the end of the table, facing the mistress. Zillah, the maid, had a little round table to herself by the wall. Unless important visitors were present, she joined freely in the conversation; but the three young men seldom opened their mouths except to shovel in food. If, by chance, they had something they thought of sufficient interest to impart, they always addressed their remarks to Miss Lane, and prefixed them by 'Ma'am'. 'Ma'am, have you heard that Squire Bushford's sold his Black Beauty?' . . . But usually, the only sound at their end of the table was that of the scraping of plates, or of a grunt of protest if one of them nudged another too suddenly. They had special cups and saucers, very large and thick, and they drank their beer out of horns, instead of glasses or mugs. There were certain small delicacies on the table which were never offered them and which they took obvious pains not to appear to notice. When they had finished their always excellent meal, one of them said 'Pardon, Ma'am,' and they all tiptoed out. Then Zillah brought in the tea-tray and Matthew stayed for a cup of tea before he, too, withdrew."

Flora Thompson, *Lark Rise to Candleford*, p 367

The horns the men drank from were beakers made from cow's horn. In 1891, in addition to John Whitton himself, there were two blacksmiths living at the forge, Frederick Plumb, aged 31, was born in Fritwell and Tom North aged 30, from Leicester, not as many as Flora suggests, but perhaps more arrived to help out after John Whitton's death. Flora's Matthew, the foreman, who was also an experienced farrier, a "bow-legged, weak-eyed little man with sandy whiskers," was based on Frederick William Plumb, who had come from Middleton Stoney, where his family worked for the Earl of Jersey, to live and work the forge as an apprentice at the age of 16 in 1875.

Details about the contents of Kezia's four bedroomed house can be found in an inventory drawn up after Kezia's death in 1898 (detailed in Appendix 2). The first bedroom contained a 4'6" stump bedstead with flock mattress and pillows and a feather bed, four blankets, a coloured quilt, Windsor chair, rush seated chair, round oak table, towel rail etc. The second bedroom had a slightly narrower wooden 4'3" bedstead, this time with a straw paliasse and coloured quilt, with better furniture including a mahogany chest of drawers, painted dressing table, mahogany night commode and two rush seated chairs etc. Both third and fourth bedrooms had wooden bedsteads with flock beds and the usual furniture.

Main street, Fringford

7. Plan of the layout of the forge and Post Office, based on a sketch by William Plumb.

8. Frederick William Plumb, left, and Thomas Deeley in the back garden of the forge, with its narrow flower-lined paths, one of which leads to the privy, the building behind Tommy. *c.*1900. (William Plumb)

The parlour was lit by Benzoline lamps and comfortably fitted out with a tapestry carpet, several tables made of oak and mahogany, a work table, easy chair and an elbow chair. Ornaments included a weather glass by Ortelli and two coloured fruits. Glass and china was stored in here.

The kitchen, lit by paraffin lamps, was the room used everyday, and to which the smiths would have access, so instead of carpet there was cocoa matting on the floor. Mrs Whitton and her staff probably ate off the oak stand table, and her servant off the two leaf oak table. There were three Windsor elbow chairs and five ordinary ones, together with a 30-hour clock in an oak case, a bureau made from mahogany and oak, a painted corner cupboard . . . The china for tea was blue and white and the teapots of block tin. The pantry was well stocked with 39 packets of cashmere soap, wine, jars of ketchup, lard, beer cans, plus a perforated meatsafe, baking tins, red earthenware pans, pewter plates, oil tins, stills and a wire egg basket.

The wash house was also used for storage, housing the salting lead and odds and ends like a fish kettle, saucepans, Bradford's mangle, wet hams and wet bacon. The entire contents of house and forge were valued at £163. 2s 9d. As the valuation was made to show what was being taken over by Frederick Plumb, who was going to rent the forge and house, some furniture and personal effects may have been removed by Kezia's son George before the inventory was made; however it bears out Flora's description of Miss Lane's house, with her taste for inherited items rather than new-fangled plush-covered suites and Japanese fans. Here she is talking about the front kitchen, which served as a living room, cooking being done in the back kitchen.:

> "So the grandfather's clock in the front kitchen still struck the hours as it had done on the day of the Battle of Waterloo. The huge, heavy oak table at the head of which she carved for the workmen and maid, sitting in higher or lower seats according to degree, was older still. There was a legend it had been made in the kitchen by the then village carpenter and was too large to remove without taking it to pieces...."

Lark Rise to Candleford, p. 364

This clock, made by John Fardon of Woodstock and Deddington, is still in the Plumb family. Flora exaggerated a little by mentioning four-poster bedsteads—perhaps she had seen the ones in the pub at Juniper Hill and was thinking back to those. One of the items acquired from the forge by the Plumbs was a book entitled *The Complete Farrier*, which Flora mentions seeing:

> "A few books, such as *Cooking and Household Management*, *The Complete Farrier*, and Dr Johnson's *Dictionary*, were kept on one of the kitchen window-seats, but all the best books were kept behind glass doors above the bureau in the parlour. When one of these was lent to Laura, it had first to be fitted with a brown-paper jacket, for Miss Lane was most particular about her books, most of which had belonged to her father."

Lark Rise to Candleford, pp. 413–4

Running the forge was as important to Kezia as running the Post Office. The low part of the building to the left of the house was used for shoeing the horses. The separate blacksmith's shop had two forges served by one

9. The frontispiece of Mrs Whitton's copy of *The Complete Farrier*, which was kept on the kitchen window seat. (John Watts)

central anvil. There was also a wheelwright's shop with a tin roof behind the house. The forge served most of the local gentry including the Chinnerys of the Manor House, the Goslings of Stratton Audley and the Harrisons of Shelswell Park.

As well as shoeing horses and doing general repairs at the forge, Frederick Plumb ('Matthew') and two assistants drove off three times a week in the spring cart to visit local hunting stables to shoe horses there.

The men were skilled at shoeing all sorts of animals, from the cart-horses to gypsy nags and even donkeys:

> "Many of the horses were very patient; but a few would plunge and kick and rear when approached. These Matthew himself shod and, under his skilful handling, they would quiet down immediately. He had only to put his hand on the mane and whisper a few words in the ear. It was probably the hand and voice which soothed them; but it was generally believed that he whispered some charm which had power over them, and he rather encouraged this idea by saying when questioned: 'I only speaks to 'em in their own language.'..."

Lark Rise to Candleford, pp. 371-2

The 1898 valuation also shows the range of equipment used in the forge. There was a blacksmith's shop which contained one pair of bellows, various tools, horseshoes and shoeing equipment, vetinerary items such as docking irons and bull ringing irons and a quantity of iron, staples etc. The second forge had another pair of bellows, described specifically as circular bellows, so perhaps the one in the blacksmith's shop was pear-shaped, more tools, horseshoes, tinman's tools, presumably used for repairing tin items, more vetinerary items such as bull's feet parers and tooth file.

In the Storeroom were quantities of wood for stales, or handles, suggesting that an important part of the work was repairing tools for local farmers (Flora wrote that the men were adept at mending not only tools but household objects). It also contained a vast quantity of various types of screws, bolts, nails, sheets of tin, hoop iron for making tyres for wagon wheels and tools and coal to fire the forges. There was another room described as a shoeing house which only contained an iron manger.

Mrs Whitton owned a bay cob, housed in her stable, to pull her spring cart, and kept four stocks of bees and a patent hive - presumably a rectangular wooden one rather than the straw bee skeps used by Sally, and stored 'outside' were items such as a pig trough, hog tub, portable forge, other blacksmith's tools and garden tools. On the grass outside the forge was a rectangular tyreing platform, on which a wagon wheel would be placed so that the red-hot iron tyre could be placed over it, then quickly doused with water to cool it down and shrink it to fit the wheel exactly. There were stores of potatoes, garden produce, wood and coal, and the remains of a rick of hay from Mrs Whitton's meadow.

Kezia Whitton died in February 1898 aged 63. Frederick Plumb had to

10. A Fringford woman in her sunbonnet. (Oxfordshire Photographic Archive)

take out the left hand upstairs bedroom window so that her heavy coffin could be laboriously lowered down a ladder, as it was too big to carry down the stairs. He had been working as a blacksmith there for more than twenty years and was able to lease the forge from the Whittons' son George. He carried on the work as blacksmith, wheelwright and farrier largely on his own, employing additional labour as and when he required it, also doing odd jobs such as repairing pots and pans. Frederick Plumb was good at tending sick animals, probably cattle as well as horses judging by the vetinerary equipment listed in the inventory, and he carried on with this work after he took over the forge.

The Post Office was moved to Rectory Lane where it was run first by James Henry Wyatt and later by Mr and Mrs Edward Price. The Plumbs purchased the property in 1923 for £500. Frederick died in 1930, and was buried in Fringford churchyard, but the forge continued in business, rented by Ernest Perrin, until he bought the other blacksmith's shop in Fringford, situated near the pub, in 1953.

Entertainments

There were few organised entertainments, apart from the Penny Readings and Church Socials, but most people turned out to watch the annual meet of the Bicester Hunt on the first Saturday in January, which met outside the Butcher's Arms on the outskirts of the village. It must have looked very colourful with the riders in their scarlet jackets, the aristocratic ladies in close-fitting habits and the excited hounds. Flora obviously sympathised with the fate of the fox, and was more interested in watching the people on the Green, as it gave her the opportunity of seeing a wide variety of the local populace:

> "The whole neighbourhood turned out to see the Meet. Both road-ways were lined with little basketwork pony-carriages with elderly ladies in furs, governess-cars with nurses and children, farm carts with forks stuck up in loads of manure, and butcher's and grocer's carts and baker's white tilted vans, and donkey-barrows in which red-faced, hoarse-shouting hawkers stood up for a better view...

11. People gathering to watch a hunt meet in North Oxfordshire, c.1900. (John Watts)

146

On the green itself school-teachers, curates, men in breeches and gaiters with ash sticks, men in ragged coats and mufflers, smartly dressed girls from Candleford town and local women in white aprons with babies in their arms pressed forward to see all there was to be seen, while older children rushed hither and thither shouting, 'Tally-ho! Tally-ho!' and only missed by a miracle being hit by the horses' hoofs."

Lark Rise to Candleford, p. 420

Fringford Feast, held annually on the village green, was another colourful occasion, although this time the clergy and aristocracy stayed away. It was a far grander occasion than the Cottisford feast, with the trappings of a small fair—swing boats, roundabouts and hurdy-gurdies as well as a myriad of stalls and activities such as shooting galleries and coconut shies. All the young people dressed in their best and crowds came out from Bicester and nearby villages. Flora once again was an onlooker, preferring to watch the goings on from her bedroom window at the forge, except for the feast to which her brother 'Edmund' escorted her and from which he was banned from the coconut shy for knocking off too many coconuts!

12. The Friendly Society procession leaving Fringford church on feast day, after the service, on their way to enjoy the entertainment on the village green, *c*.1900–10. (William Plumb)

It was occasions such as this which gave her the chance to appreciate some of the local colour of the area, later used as some of the raw material for her writing. As she grew in confidence she realised that she did not want to spend all her life in the one small area where she was unlikely to get advancement. So in 1897 she gave in her notice, probably went to Twyford for a while, took a series of temporary jobs and finally a permanent one at Grayshott in Surrey.

9

Brackley, Banbury, Bicester, and Buckingham: Flora's Candleford

ℬℯ

"Candleford was but a small town and their cousins' home was on the outskirts ... To Laura it was both town and country and in that lay part of its charm. It was thrilling, after being used to walking miles to buy a reel of cotton or a packet of tea, to be able to dash out without a hat to fetch something from a shop for her aunt; and still more thrilling to spend whole sunny mornings gazing into shop windows with her cousins. There were such marvellous thing in the Candleford shops, such as the wax lady dressed in the height of fashion, with one of the new bustles, at the leading draper's, and the jeweller's window, sparkling with gold and silver and gems, and the toy shops and the sweet shops, and, above all, the fishmonger's where a whole salmon reposed on a bed of green reeds with ice sprinkled over (ice in August! They would never believe it at home), and an aquarium with live gold-fish swimming round and round stood round near the desk where they took your money."

Lark Rise to Candleford, p. 340

This is an amorphous description which could apply to many places and typifies why Candleford is perhaps the most difficult place to tie down in detail, although Buckingham is where Flora said her uncle 'James Dowland' lived. Flora knew several towns which could have formed the basis for her 'Candleford'.

1. Brackley market place with the town hall in the centre. (John Watts)

Brackley

As a child she would certainly have often visited Brackley, just over the Northamptonshire border, and she and her family did their shopping there, although there are surprisingly few direct references to it in *Lark Rise to Candleford*. Her father, Albert Timms, worked there for a builder whose yard was on the Banbury Road, behind a house called The Statuaries, where the builder himself lived. In later life this building was used as the headquarters for the Conservative Club and more recently the yard has been turned into a new housing estate.

Brackley is a small, quiet town, based around the market square, which reached the height of its prosperity in the early middle ages, when there was a castle just to the south along the Hinton road. Because the town has not developed greatly, there are still many traces of the medieval planned borough, including street names indicating trades such as Market Street, Butcher's Row, Saltersgate, Cook Row and Souter Row (shoemaker's row). The town gradually declined from the late middle ages, and not even the opening of the L.N.W.R. Bletchley to Banbury railway with a station at Brackley made much impact on the town. Later another station was opened when the G.W.R. built the Leicester to Marylebone line. Both railway lines have now closed.

Although Brackley was small, there was a wide range of occupations in the late nineteenth century. The main industry was brewing and there were lots of different shops from drapers and milliners, pillow lace manufacturers, straw hat maker, watchmaker and jewellers, tailors, boot and shoemaker, china and glass dealer, a fancy repository and Berlin wool depot, bookseller to fishmonger and poulterer, butcher, grocer and haberdasher, baker, confectioner, chemist and druggist and fruiterer. There were also occupations connected with farming such as woodman and farmer, corn miller, saddler, land surveyor, harness maker and shoeing and jobbing smith, plus of course builders. A market was held each Wednesday and a wool fair in June with ordinary fairs in October and December. The population in 1881 was 2504.

Although Flora makes few direct references to the town, another indication of the connection her family had with Brackley comes from the books of the Rock of Hope Lodge of the I.A.A.F. Manchester Unity Friendly Society in Brackley. Albert Timms belonged to this and the secretary was a local builder, Alan Wootton, which possibly suggests that he was Albert's

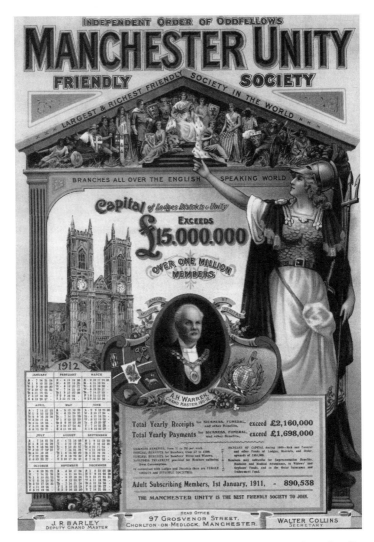

2. Calendar of the Independent Order of Oddfellows, the Friendly Society to which Albert Timms belonged. (John Watts)

employer, but as he was based in the High Street, and the yard where Albert worked was in the Banbury Road it is not yet possible to be definite about this. Albert was contracted to pay in a regular sum each month, and would then receive sick benefits and funeral expenses. There are references to him drawing sick pay of 2s with 6d for incidentals on 16 March 1886, the same on 6th June 1887, six shillings and sixpence on 12 March 1888 and two shillings and sixpence on 17 December 1888 and notes of the amount of money he paid into the Society. It is interesting that some months he did not pay his 2s 6d contribution, having to pay a larger sum later to make up for what he had missed - this echoes what Flora wrote about his attitude to money. A reference in *Still Glides the Stream* to Charity's father visiting the Oddfellows Benefit Club in 'Mixlow' could well refer to Albert Timms:

"The fourteenth of each month was her father's club night, when he walked into Mixlow to pay his subscription to the Oddfellows Benefit Club, and usually, as he said, made a night of it, meaning that he might not be home before eleven o'clock, a late hour at Restharrow. When he came home he would be gay and animated, not from what he had drunk, for he seldom took more than one pint of ale, but because the talk at the club had been stimulating. Members of other, more conventional fraternities used at that time to say that the Oddfellows were not better than a lot of old freemasons, and this idea was not discouraged by the Oddfellows themselves. Though their mysteries probably consisted of no more than a password to gain admittance to their clubroom, the addressing each other as 'Brother' while there, and the possession of an elected member known as 'our almoner', whose office it was to visit the sick and dispense benefits, they liked to think of their own as a secret society. In politics, the majority of the brethren were Liberals with a Radical tinge; many of them were less strict churchgoers than their neighbours - one man belonging to the Mixlow branch professed to be an atheist—and altogether, the Oddfellows were regarded as a daring lot; though, strange as it may have appeared to some people, their lives were generally exemplary."

Still Glides the Stream, pp. 159–60

Banbury

Banbury was a much larger town, which is, unusually, mentioned several times by its real name in *Still Glides the Stream*. Flora could have travelled there by train or by carriers' cart. The first reference concerns Stella Pocock, who considers herself a cut above her neighbours and talks disparagingly about the pompadour aprons made for Charity and her cousins, largely because she did not have one herself:

3. The Statuaries, the house in Brackley belonging to the builder who employed Albert Timms, which is situated next to the site of his builders' yard (now a housing estate) on the Banbury road.

"They were getting common, she said; the last time she and her mother were in Banbury they had seen a gipsy selling clothes-pegs in an apron very like Bess's." (p. 90)

Later in the book, Charity Finch, the heroine, has just been awarded the status of full pupil teacher and wants to spend the precious sovereign she has been given as a reward in Banbury, with her cousin Bess,

"for she dearly loved a trip into Banbury in the carrier's cart to see the shops and to enjoy a cup of tea at Bett's." (p. 125).

A few pages letter she thinks of the trip she has not been able to take because she had undertaken an urgent secret errand for Bess:

"If her mother were thinking of her at that moment, she would picture her with Bess, gazing into shop windows, or sipping tea and nibbling a Banbury cake in the Old Teashop." (p. 130).

Flora wrote to Leslie Castle several times about Banbury, which she had remembered from her childhood as being a quiet country town:

"I had always thought of it in connection with the fighting in the Civil War and the Puritan hanging the cat on Monday for catching a mouse on Sunday and of Banbury Cross and, all the time, it has been growing into a large industrial town. I went there several times in the carrier's cart as a child and had that place partly in mind when creating my Candleford, though most of our relations lived in Buckingham."

Letter dated 24 February 1945

Banbury, famous for its cakes since the sixteenth century, was a much bigger market town than Brackley, with a population of 9660 in 1881, although like Brackley it still retains much of its medieval plan. St Mary's church stands in Horsefair, up the road from the Victorian Banbury cross, with the High Street leading down to the market place on one side of it, and Parson's Street forming the other side of a triangle linking them. The Saxon settlement was turned into a planned town by Bishop Alexander of Lincoln in the 12th century, and it became the second most important town in Oxfordshire, after Oxford itself. Its main industry at the beginning of the Victorian period was weaving plush, different types of which were used for purposes as diverse as liveries for the courts of the world, panning gold in South Africa, Japanese winter kimonos, friction gloves, photography, and embossed plush specially made for furnishings in the House of Commons, the House of Lords and the Reform Club as well as for private houses such as Broughton Castle.

Later in the century plush came second to the industry of agricultural engineering. The foundations of this were laid in Banbury by James Gardner, who patented a turnip cutter in 1834. In 1848 his business was purchased by Bernhard Samuelson, whose engineering works in Tours had been closed down by the 1848 revolution. He set up the Britannia Works on three sites near the railway station, and built a variety of machines, including the American McCormick reaping machines under licence. It may well have been Samuelson's machines that were beginning to appear in Flora's countryside:

"After the Jubilee nothing ever seemed quite the same. The old Rector died and the farmer, who had seemed immovable except by death, had to retire to make way for the heir of the landowning nobleman who intended to farm the family estates himself. He brought with him the new self-binding reaping machine and women were no longer required in the harvest field."

Lark Rise to Candleford, p. 246

Other occupations in Banbury included printing, basket making, straw plaiting, chair-making, coopering, tailoring, cork burning, clay pipe making, mop-making, leather crafts, tanning and narrow boat building.

It was the Banbury cakes that Flora remembered about the town—she made another reference to them in Candleford Green when she had her first tea at the Post Office:

"It seemed a pity to Laura that the first time she had been offered two eggs at one meal she could barely eat one and that the Banbury cake, hitherto to her a delicious rarity only seen in her home when purchased by visiting aunts, should flake and crumble almost untasted upon her plate because she felt too excited and anxious to eat."

Lark Rise to Candleford, p. 397

4. Advertisement for Mrs E.W.Brown's Banbury Cake Shop in Parson's Street. Flora makes several references to enjoying Banbury cakes in her book. (Oxfordshire County Libraries)

E. W. BROWN,
The Original Cake Shop.
A.D. 1638.
12, *Parson's Street*, Banbury.

E. W. BROWN wishes it to be distinctly noted that all ingredients used in the manufacture of these Goods are of the finest and purest quality.

WEDDING CAKES,
Superior in quality and design, made to order; full particulars on application to E. W. BROWN.

Wedding Cakes
From 5/- to £20 each.
PACKED AND SENT TO ANY PART OF THE WORLD.

Christening and Birthday Cakes
Iced and Ornamented with Mottoes, Monograms, etc.

ORDERS BY POST CAREFULLY ATTENDED TO.
Carriage Paid on all Parcels by Rail of 5/- value and upwards

5. Engraving of the Original Cake Shop run by the Brown family in Parson's Street, Banbury, from Alfred Beesley's *History of Banbury*, 1841.

6. Silhouette of Betty White, renowned 18th century maker of Banbury cakes, from Alfred Beesley's *History of Banbury*, 1841.

7. The Betts' Banbury Cake Shop in the High Street, Banbury, *c*.1878 (Oxfordshire Photographic Archive)

Banbury cakes now have a rich fruit filling in a pastry crust. The first reference to them came in Thomas Bright's *Treatise of Melancholie* in 1586:

> "Sodden wheat is a grosse and melancholicke nourishment and bread especially of the fine flower [flour] unleavened. Of this sort are bag puddings made with flower, fritters, pancakes. such as we call Banberrie Cakes, and the great ones are confected with butter, eggs, etc., used at weddings, and however it be prepared rye and bread made thereof carried with it plenty of melancholie."

They had a dubious reputation in the seventeenth century too, when Ben Johnson, the playwright made his Puritan character Zeal-of-the-Land Busy, a baker, (who may have been based on the Banbury baker Richard Busby) give up his baking because his Banbury cakes were served at such pagan ceremonies as bride ales, may day and morris dances. The Original Cake shop was in Parson's Street from the seventeenth century, almost opposite the Reindeer Inn.

The owners in the eighteenth century included Betty and Jarvis White. Betty was said to be an excellent and careful baker who was jealous of her good reputation: "My name is quiet Betty, I never meddles nor makes with anybody, no mealman never calls on me twice." she would say. When people commented on the high price of her cakes she explained "Only think, there's currans, they be twice the price th' used to be, and then there's butter an' sugar they be double the price th' was formerly." Jarvis was rather fonder of leaning over the shop door and promoting her cakes than actually doing any work. He maintained that the cakes were so light that a sparrow could fly off with one in its beak. In the late nineteenth century Mrs Brown was running the Original Cake Shop, and Banbury cakes were also baked by William Betts in his half-timbered shop in the High Street and by Daniel Claridge in Parson's Street. The cakes had a world-wide reputation, being exported as far as America and Australia. The Cake Shop which Flora knew was demolished in 1969, but items relating to Banbury cakes can be seen in Banbury Museum.

Flora makes another reference to Banbury in relation to Queenie the lacemaker, who made lace all the year ready to take it to sell at Banbury fair:

> "Them wer' the days!' she would sigh. 'Money to spend.' And she would tell of the bargains she had bought with her earnings. Good brown calico and linsey-woolsey, and a certain chocolate print

sprigged with white, her favourite gown, of which she could still show a pattern in her big patchwork quilt. Then there was a fairing to be bought for those at home—pipes and packets of shag tobacco for the men, rag dolls and ginger-bread for the little 'uns', and snuff for the old grannies. And the home-coming, loaded with treasure, and money in the pocket besides. Tripe. They always bought tripe; it was the only time in the year they could get it, and it was soon heated up, with onions and a nice bit of thickening, and after supper there was hot, spiced elderberry wine, and so to bed, everybody happy.

Now, of course, things were different. She didn't know what the world was coming to. This nasty machine-made stuff had killed the lace-making; the dealer had not been to the Fair for the last ten years ..."

Lark Rise to Candleford, p. 84

Banbury Michaelmas Fair was quite an occasion in the nineteenth century, with people travelling long distances to visit it as there were few organised entertainments then, apart from those provided at fairs. As many agricultural labourers were employed on a yearly contract, which ended after the harvest, they would leave the farm, have a few days holiday and visit the local hiring fair to find a new job. There were many stalls selling items as

8. Ticket for Banbury Mechanics' Institute. Such organisations gave working people the opportunity to continue their education after leaving school, and ran lending libraries. Flora borrowed books from the free reading room in Bicester which had the same aims. (Oxfordshire County Libraries)

diverse as ribbons, shawls, toys and dolls, gingerbread and Banbury cakes, plus entertainments such as a camera obscura, a wild west show, swing boats, helter skelter, ferris wheel, haunted house and later steam yachts and bioscopes. The town hummed with people and it was a happy time for the crowds.

Bicester

Flora would have visited Bicester when she lived at Fringford, and it bears much resemblance to the 'Mixlow' of *Still Glides the Stream*, although that also contains elements of Brackley. It was almost certainly the post town referred to when trying to identify the writer of the anonymous letters:

> "Charity examined the postmark. It was that of Mixlow, their own post town. All the letters written at Restharrow and handed to the postman bore that postmark, as well as those posted in the town and in other villages for miles around."
>
> *Still Glides the Stream*, p. 126

In 1881 the population of Bicester was 3306. It was a small market town, which according to *Kelly's Directory of Oxfordshire* for 1887 was famous for the purity of its water and its beer. There had been a Roman town called Alchester close to the town, and Bicester had a Saxon settlement, some suggesting that its name was derived from St. Birinus, the first Bishop of Dorchester on Thames, who converted the area to Christianity. A more orthodox explanation is that the name derives from 'Bernecestre', 'the fort of the warriors' or 'of Beorna'.

The town has several nuclei which developed in the middle ages: King's End is traditionally the site of the original town, possibly founded by St. Birinus and later destroyed by marauding Danes, which formed part of the royal manor of Kirtlington, hence its name. It was granted around the twelfth century to the nuns of Markyate Priory near Luton, Bedfordshire, who built a manor house and grange on the site of the present Bicester House. When the priory was dissolved in 1536 John Coker acquired the land and extended the house, enclosing a small park around it. In 1634 grant of arms was made by heralds visiting Oxfordshire to Cadwallader Coker, an ancestor of the vicar of the same name whom Flora knew in Fringford, who came from Bicester.

Market End, which was called Bury End until about 1542, has the triangular market square at its centre. The charter granting a market was issued in the 1239 to William de Longespee.

A third area grew up round the Saxon church, dedicated to the Virgin Mary and St Edburg, named after the daughter of Edward the Elder, and the Causeway, midway between King's End and Market End. Very little remains of Saxon work as the church was largely rebuilt in the twelfth century and enlarged over the next three hundred years. An Augustinian Priory was built south east of the church, endowed by Gilbert Bassett in 1182–5 for a prior and eleven canons.

Well established crafts in the nineteenth century included wool-combing, straw plaiting, lace, rope, sack-cloth and basket making, and leather slippers. *Kelly's Directory* for 1887 shows continuity, with John and Eliza Barrett making rope and twine, a tanner and currier, several boot and shoe makers and a basketmaker. Bicester had the usual variety of shops and other trades included seedsmen, brewers and mineral water manufacturers, and a commercial traveller.

Flora would have known little of the early history of the town, but was aware of some aspects of life there from her childhood. She tells the story of a retired bachelor, 'Mr Sharman', nicknamed 'the Major', who lived on his own, keeping his little house neat and tidy until he became old and weak. Emma Timms helped to care for him when he was ill; then he spent a few weeks in hospital in Oxford. When he returned he brought small presents for the children—a set of doll's dishes with food for Flora and a tin engine for Edwin, plus a silk handkerchief for Emma, a pipe for Albert and a rattle for the baby, which were received with delight. Emma carried on taking him food, and doing what she could, but eventually it was clear that he could no longer manage on his own, and the doctor had to call in the relieving officer and organise for him to be taken to the workhouse infirmary:

" They were right in their decision, He was not able to look after himself; he had no relatives or friends able to undertake the responsibility; the workhouse was the best place for him. But they made one terrible mistake. They were dealing with a man of intelligence, and spirit, and they treated him as they might have done one in the extreme of senile decay. They did not consult him or tell him what they had decided; but ordered the carrier's cart to call at his house the next morning and wait at a short distance while they, in the doctor's gig, drove up to his door. When they entered, the Major had just dressed and dragged himself to his chair by the fire. 'It's a nice morning, and we've come to take you for a drive,' announced the doctor cheerfully, and in spite of his protests, they hustled on his coat and had him out and in the carrier's cart in a very few minutes.

Laura saw the carrier touch up his horse with the whip and the cart turn, and she always wished afterwards she had not, for, as soon as he realized where he was being taken, the old soldier, the independent old bachelor, the kind family friend, collapsed and cried like a child. He was beaten, but not for long. Before six weeks were over he was back in the parish and all his troubles were over, for he came in his coffin."

Lark Rise to Candleford, pp. 89–90

He would have been taken to the Bicester Union Workhouse, which was built just off George Street, Highfield in Bicester in 1836 to accommodate 350 inmates. To be sent to the workhouse was a fate that elderly people dreaded. Husbands and wives were separated, life was degradingly institutionalised and hard, and they would do anything they could to avoid it.

9. Bicester Union Workhouse, which opened in 1836, catering for the poor of 38 parishes. Most people only went to the workhouse when they were absolutely desperate, as conditions there were often degrading. (John Watts)

10. Dr C.M.Hendriks, the inspiration for Flora's 'Dr. Henderson', taken from his obituary in the Bicester Advertiser. (John Watts)

'Dr Henderson' is mentioned in Candleford Green as living on the green, but according to directories there was no doctor in Fringford and he was probably based on the character of Dr Hendriks who lived in London Road Bicester, near the junction with Market Hill, practising with Dr Cotterell from 1885 before buying the practice in 1890. Flora wrote that he lived in a long low brown house with a red lamp outside. He had a loud bell, and people trying to contact him at night had to shout up to him through a speaking tube. Although he did not like being roused from his bed, and had a tendency to swear about it while harnessing his horse, he was noted for his excellent bedside manner.

When describing her first arrival in Candleford, Flora wrote a description that could well apply to Bicester, and Dr Hendriks' house:

"Candleford seemed a very large and grand place to Laura, with its several large streets meeting in a square where there were many large shop windows, with the blinds drawn because it was Sunday, and a doctor's house with a red lamp over the gate, and a church with a tall spire..."

Lark Rise to Candleford, p. 305

Dr Hendriks was a dapper man with a pointed beard, sporting an eyeglass, who wore white spats and a light waistcoat and carried a silver-headed cane. His obituary in the *Bicester Advertiser* on 24 July 1925 described him as a genial man who gave fatherly care to his patients:

"Wherever he could do good, he did it without ostentation. A life such as his will be sadly missed, for it may with truth be said of him that he lived and moved and gave his life and talents for others. He had either a kind word or a joke for everyone. His heart was so sympathetic that his patients' sorrows and troubles he made his own. He would give the last ounce of his strength if it would benefit the sufferer... His death came as a profound shock to the inhabitants of Bicester, and the people of the countryside will miss the pleasant figure so frequently seen in and out amongst them helping and advising."

One of his public offices was that of medical officer for Bicester Post Office, and Flora may have met him in this context. According to local lore, he was a generous man who often neglected to present his bills to his patients when he knew that they would find them difficult to pay. However he noted down the fees in a book, which after his death was found by his executors, who, to the horror of the local people, sent out all the bills. Dr. Hendrik's generosity is mentioned in *Still Glides the Stream* (page 96):

"The old doctor at Mixlow, who attended the country people for miles around that town and to quite half his patients sent in no bill because he knew that they were too poor to pay one, about the time when pompadour aprons first appeared instituted what was known as a Doctor's Club, the members of which paid twopence weekly and, for that, when ill, were entitled to free attendance. When this club had been long enough in existence for the members to claim benefits, there was such an outbreak of minor ailments that he had to engage... an assistant..."

Another Bicester institution Flora mentioned was a Mechanics' Institute

11. Staff of Bicester Post Office, *c.* 1900. The postmaster Walter Joseph French (Flora's 'Mr Rushton') sits in the centre with Miss Wrapson on the left and Miss Toovey on the right. The women were described by Flora as the two daughters of a minister, quiet, refined women in their thirties. As they never married, there was no vacancy for Flora at Bicester Post Office. (John Watts)

where she was encouraged by Mrs Whitton to borrow books to read. There was a Mechanics' Institute in Banbury, founded by Sir Bernhard Samuelson, which now houses the public library in Marlborough Road. The equivalent in Bicester was a free reading room for labouring men, endowed by the Earl of Jersey, which opened in 1872, offering them newspapers, and presumably books to read.

Flora's uncle 'James Dowland' is very difficult to identify, and is unlikely to have lived in Bicester, but there was a builder there who may have been one of the inspirations for the character: Joseph Belsey Layton, a cabinet maker. At the age of 23 he married Miss C.E.Bricknell, who was 12 years older than he was, in Finsbury, London, in 1872, and took over her dealership in china, glass and earthenware in Bicester, later extending the business to become a builders' merchant. He was listed in the 1887 Kelly's Directory as an upholsterer and china dealer in Market Hill, but he and his son George were the biggest builders in Bicester. They were never listed as builders in the Directories as they did not sell the houses, or build for other people, instead renting out their properties. In the early 1890s they started to build thirteen houses in Bath Terrace, eight houses in Manchester

12. Market Hill, Bicester *c*.1905. It is reminiscent of Flora's description of Candleford having several streets meeting in a square where the blinds were drawn over the shop windows as it was Sunday. Dr Hendriks, probably Flora's 'Dr Henderson', lived in the house on the left before the elm tree. (John Watts)

13. Joseph Belsay Layton (1849–1901) and his son George Layton (1878–1954) with some of their staff in the builders' yard behind Layton's shop on Market Hill, Bicester, in 1883. The staff are, from left to right: unknown, Joseph Grantham, staircase maker, man with pole: Arthur Edward Waine (1863–1947), stonemason and first cousin of Albert Timms, boy behind him may be a member of the Simons family, man with watch-chain is foreman James Small, small boy in suit is George Layton, man in top hat with watch-chain is Joseph Belsay Layton himself, two unknown men, extreme right Thomas Edward Waine (1846–1918), another cousin of Albert Timms, who later became a wheelwright in Launton. (David Watts)

Terrace and a further eight houses, all in Victoria Road. Around 1900 they built seven large villa-style houses in London Road, some of which have black and white tiled paths like those described by Flora. Nineteen houses were also built in Field Street on the Fringford side of the town and Joseph himself moved into number seven which has since been divided into two houses. The description of Laura's arrival in Candleford at her uncle's house could apply to the house with the hooded front door and a post and chain fence in Market Hill owned by Joseph Layton:

"But they were pulling up at a tall white house set back on a little green with a chestnut tree supporting scaffold poles and ladders and a sign which informed the public that James Dowland, Builder and Contractor, was ready and competent to undertake 'Constructions, Renovations and Sanitary Work. Estimates Free.'

14. Market Hill, Bicester, c.1900, showing Joseph Layton's house and the shop they ran from the 1870s until the 1950s. Flora describes 'Uncle James Dowland's' house as probably being Georgian, and in the centre of town. (John Watts)

15. London Road, Bicester. The houses on the left were built at the turn of the century by Joseph Belsay Layton. (John Watts)

Readers have no doubt noticed how seldom builders live in houses of their own construction ... Uncle James Dowland's house was probably Georgian. The eight windows with their clinging wreaths of wistaria were beautifully spaced and the flight of steps which led up to the hooded front door was guarded by the low white posts and chains which enclosed the little green."

Lark Rise to Candleford, p. 305

16. Grimsley's fish shop in Sheep Street, Bicester, with the shop assistants (the one on the right is Flora's second cousin Jack Waine, who lived from 1896–1962), proudly displaying a 203lb halibut. In one of her descriptions of Candleford Flora marvelled over:

"The fishmonger's where a whole salmon reposed on a bed of green reeds with ice sprinkled over (ice in August! They would never believe it at home) ..."

Lark Rise to Candleford, p. 340. (John Watts)

Flora gives a detailed description of 'Uncle James', an important looking man:

> "Uncle James was so tall and stout and dark, with eyebrows so bushy and so thick a moustache, with so glossy a Sunday suit and so heavy a gold watchchain that, before him, the others present seemed to fade into the background."
>
> (pp. 305–6)

This is similar to the photograph of Joseph Layton except that the latter has side whiskers and a beard. Joseph's son George was also a highly respected man in Bicester. He lived in a mansion he built in London Road and in 1912 built Layton's Garage in London Road, from which he sold cars to the gentry. He became Chairman of Bicester Urban District Council in 1920 and was the first tradesman in Bicester to become a magistrate.

Buckingham

Flora always maintained that Buckingham was the main influence for her depiction of Candleford. It is the county town of Buckinghamshire, although now overtaken in prominence and size by the likes of Aylesbury and Milton Keynes, so that, like Brackley, the town retains its old-world character. It has its origins in the Anglo-Saxon period, the first mention of it being in 915AD when Edward the Elder had it fortified for protection against the Danes. It grew in the middle ages because of the wool trade and received a royal charter in the sixteenth century. In the centre of the town is Castle Hill, which housed a Norman castle, where tradition says Hereward was imprisoned. The ruined castle was obliterated by the building of the parish church in the late eighteenth century, only the mound remaining. However by the 16th century Buckingham was in decline. Perhaps because of this, it retains some early elements such as St John the Baptist's chapel, a small stone building with a tiled roof, on Market Hill, which dates partly from the late twelfth century, with fifteenth century alterations such as a traceried window and truss roof, made when it was converted into a Latin School by Edward VI. Not to be outdone, Queen Elizabeth founded Christ's Hospital for seven poor women. The High Street has some sixteenth and seventeenth century houses. In the seventeenth century there were several craft guilds in the town, which indicated the principal manufactures: the Mercers, Apothecaries, Chandlers, Clothiers, Goldsmiths, Grocers, Haberdashers, Hat and

17. The Sheep Fair in the High Street, Buckingham, *c*.1900, looking towards the Old Gaol. (Buckinghamshire County Museum)

Cap Makers, Ironmongers, Linen Drapers, Mercers, Salters, Silkmen and Woollen Drapers; the Cordwainers included Collar-makers, Girdle-makers, Glovers, Parchment Makers, Poynters and Poyntmakers, Saddlers, Shoemakers and Tanners; the Tailors' Guild included Brasiers, Dyers, Fletchers, Furbishers, Fullers, Glaziers, Painters, Pewterers, Tailors and Weavers; the Butchers' Guild included Bakers, Brewers, Butchers, Cooks and Millers.

There was a disastrous fire in the town in 1725, so many Georgian houses were built to replace earlier ones are found. Some earlier buildings survived including the seventeenth or early eighteenth-century town hall, Castle House and the Manor House. The Gaol, built in 1748, stands to the north east of the Market Square, decorated with turrets and embattled parapets.

Even in the nineteenth century it was a country town, with a population of 3,585 in 1881, closely linked with its agricultural hinterland. Local crafts included lacemaking—Buckinghamshire lace was the finest made in the East Midlands—but the industry declined rapidly after lace-making machines were developed in Nottingham, producing much cheaper lace from the 1850s. Principal industries were brewing, malting and milling. Apart from the usual range of shops and industries, the 1887 directory mentions a manufacturer of waterproof oil sheets, a junior reporter, Bucks Direct Dairy Supply Company, a coach builder, a tinman, a livery stable keeper, a music warehouse and a hurdle maker.

Flora's grandfather Thomas Timms and his wife Martha lived in the Mitre Street section of the Gawcott Road on the outskirts of Buckingham, and Flora wrote to Leslie Castle that she visited them regularly as a child. She also had cousins, the Waines, who lived close by in Mitre Street, which would tally with the description Flora gave of her cousins living on the edge of town.

John Waine, who was born in 1842 in Launton, was a cousin of Albert and another possible candidate for the role of 'James Dowland'. He was the eldest son of Clementina Wallington, Martha's sister, and John Waine who was born in North Leigh, but farmed in Launton from 1842-55, and after that became a labourer. He and Clementina had six other sons and a daughter. John Waine junior was a stone mason, who worked for Henry Harrison, monumental mason, who operated at different times from Cow Fair, High Street, Ford Street and Hunter Street in Buckingham. He was a superb craftsman, working on churches throughout England, especially in the Oxford region, specialising in flower and animal sculpture. The cemetery in Brackley Road, Buckingham has a number of gravestones carved between 1890 and 1930 with his trade-mark flowers, almost certainly carved by him. He carried on working into his eighties and even carved his own gravestone, which is decorated with three dimensional flowers including a rose, lily of the valley and fern leaves. He specialised in carving a Celtic type cross, one of which can be seen on the top of St Bernadine's Convent, London Road, Buckingham, which was built from 1892-4. Perhaps there was a little of him in the stonemason Thomas Hearne of *Still Glides the Stream* (p. 26):

> "Hearne had in his day been a first-class workman with experience, skill, and that something beyond skill which is a compound of taste and imagination. His firm had valued his services. When there had been a difficult or a delicate job to be done, it had been given to Hearne as a matter of course. Specimens of his workmanship stood, and some must still be standing, all over that countryside, in the renovated stonework of restored churches, the arches of bridges. stone piers at entrance gates, and on the facades of mansions."

18. Photograph taken at the wedding of Flora's second cousin Harriet Clementina Waine to James Edward Blencowe on 29 August 1899. Back row, left to right: Harry Wallington Waine (1878–1948),unknown, Harriet Clementina Waine, (born 1872). Middle row: Elizabeth Waine, (born 1874), and James Edward Blencowe, labourer from Southfields, Wandsworth with his sister who is seated in front. (David Watts)

On 8 July 1869 John married Elizabeth Fenemore, a widow, the daughter of butcher John Giles, in Buckingham. They had three children: Harriet Clementina, born in 1872, Elizabeth who was baptised on 13 September 1874 and Harry Wallington Waine, baptised on 21 July 1878. The ages of the girls would fit in with the well dressed cousins Ethel and Alma, whose clothes were passed down to Flora, although admittedly there is no refer-ence in the book to a brother, and the girls did not go up in the world as much as she suggested, Elizabeth having an illegitimate daughter and Harriet marrying a labourer of Southfields, Wandsworth:

"The hats were exactly alike and the feathers of the same fullness down to the last strand. The white embroidered muslin dresses they wore were also replicas of each other for it was the fashion then to dress sisters alike, regardless of type. But the girls had seen them and came running towards the spring cart with a twinkle of long, black-stockinged legs and shiny patent-leather best shoes... Alma was twelve and Ethel thirteen, but their cool, grown-up manner might have belonged to twenty-five and thirty."

Lark Rise to Candleford, pp 303–4

In the 1881 census the family lived in Mitre Street, Buckingham. In 1899 Harriet Clementina lived at 6 Mitre Street and her brother at number 13. It is probable that the Timms and Waine families would have known one another, both because of their close relationship, and the fact that both men were stonemasons. John's success, compared to Albert's decline in the trade could account for the evident antagonism between the two, and their differences of opinion. John was a morose character, and rather particular and fussy. He could well have had a dislike of alcohol, as did 'James Dowland', because his father was reputed to have drunk away his fortune. He was an active man who claimed to walk round Buckingham four times a day, even in old age, and walked to Launton every Sunday to visit his brother Thomas who was a wheelwright there. He died in 1930, and was buried in Buckingham.

19. Mitre Street, Buckingham looking west from the bottom of Bone Hill. The Timms family lived on the left at number 15 or nearby, and their Waine cousins opposite at number 6. (David Watts)

The search for the real Candleford is a frustrating one, as the identification of Uncle Tom as Thomas Whiting who lived in Twyford, not Buckingham, means that there are few references which can definitely be ascribed to Candleford itself, and it seems most likely that it was a mixture of places—Flora herself wrote that she had been far less specific in her writing after *Lark Rise*.

10

Grayshott

ℰ

"One hot September afternoon near the end of the last century a girl of about twenty walked without knowing it over the border from Hampshire into one of its neighbouring counties. She was dressed in a brown woollen frock with a waist-length cape of the same material and a brown beaver hat decorated with two small ostrich tips, set upright in front, back to back, like a couple of notes of interrogation. This outfit, which would no doubt appear hideous to modern eyes, had given her great moral support on her train journey. The skirt, cut short just to escape contact with the ground and so needing no holding up except in wet weather, was, her dressmaker had assured her, the latest idea for country wear. The hat she had bought on her way through London that morning. It had cost her nine and eleven-pence three farthings of the pound she had saved to meet her expenses until her first month's salary was due in her new post . . . she had special reasons for wishing to make a good impression today, for she had lately been somewhat unsettled through taking short holiday-relief engagements at the post offices where she had worked and this new position, she hoped, would prove a permanency. Her people at home were beginning to speak of her as a rolling stone, and rolling stones were not in favour with country people of that day."

Heatherley, pp. 153–4

Thus Flora began the continuation of her 'autobiography', which remained unpublished until included in *A Country Calendar* in 1979. This takes her away from Oxfordshire, to the village of Grayshott, near Haslemere, on the Surrey-Hampshire border. Ironically, although she stayed there only until 1901, she came back to the same area when her husband was appointed sub-postmaster at Liphook in 1916.

Grayshott was then a modern village, which at that time was still a hamlet of Headley. The name *Gravesetta* occurs in a document of 1185 and *Grave-schete* in a Bishop's Register of 1200, signifying a clearing in a wood. The land was enclosed in 1859, and the site that became the village had been sold in 1851 to defray the expenses of the Inclosure Commissioners. Part of this land, the Grayshott Park Estate, was purchased by Edward l'Anson, who built Heather Lodge. This house was later sold to Mr Vertue, becoming the centre for the local Catholic community and eventually the Convent of the Centacle. The largest house in the village was Grayshott Hall, largely rebuilt in the 1890s of local stone dressed with red brick tiles, with its own lodge. It was renamed Grayshott Hall Farm and owned by A. Ingram Whitaker, J.P., who had married Berthe de Pury, grand-daughter of Edward l'Anson in 1895. He was a public spirited man who contributed much to the development of Grayshott. Flora probably had him in mind in describing 'Mr Doddington', who was informally thought of as 'squire'. He was a kind employer and helped those who were sick or in trouble The other houses in the area were those of squatters and fugitives from justice—ironically similar to Juniper Hill at the time of enclosure, as they were considered a rough lot who would prevent Heather Lodge from being completed. The area was far from safe, as related in *Frensham Then and Now* (Baker and Minchin, 1938), where the author described how his father was returning home from Haslemere Fair after selling some cattle:

"It was now dusk. Immediately on entering Wagner's Wells Bottom I passed a drove of ponies lying down in the fern, and had only proceeded a few hundred yards when I heard a shrill whistle from my rear. Startled by the sound, the ponies I had just passed came galloping down on me. At once I realised that I had been marked down at the Fair. As they overtook me I managed to grasp one of them by his mane and neck and ran beside him. Almost immediately I saw figures emerging from the high furze bushes which grew densely in the narrowest part of the valley. But with the ponies all round me I broke through them safely and reached Simmondstone sound in limb and pocket. I learnt afterwards that the gang who waylaid me were from Blackdown, over the Sussex border ... It was the custom of the Blackdown Gang to work Hindhead, while Hindhead went further afield."

The village was big enough to warrant a postal service in 1867, although all the post was delivered to Edward l'Anson's house for collection from there. The village shop opened in Henry Robinson's Mount Cottage in the 1870s. He sold this house to Edward l'Anson, moving into Crossways (then known as Hindhead Road). People used to collect their letters from his new shop there, and it became the Post Office in 1887.

The population of Grayshott increased rapidly in the latter part of the nineteenth century, from 100 in 1872 to 666 in 1901, when there were 143 houses. As the Hindhead area was considered particularly healthy it attracted visitors in the summer. In *Kelly's Directory of Hampshire* for 1899 various shops and businesses are listed in Grayshott, revealing far more shops and businesses than Flora would have found in the villages she knew in Oxfordshire, including a fruiterer, beer retailer, draper, grocer and wine and spirit merchant, tobacconist, fishmonger, 2 butchers, greengrocer, baker and confectioner, draper and bookseller, ironmonger, dress maker, launderer. saddler, 2 boot makers, physician, fly proprietor, cycle agent, builder and blacksmith. It was to the Post Office where Walter Chapman operated as a carpenter, joiner, builder, cabinet maker and stationer that Flora came. This was situated in what is now Crossways (but the building was demolished in 1986 and replaced by a block of two shops). Many of the buildings Flora knew are still there, including the shops near the Post Office built in the late nineteenth century with red tile-hanging. The village was described in 1898 by Thomas Wright in *Hindhead*:

" . . . Grayshott . . . consists of a street of spruce looking shops situated near a spot where five roads meet, and a number of handsome private residences and palatial lodging houses dotted about in the remains of a forest of glorious larches and Scotch pines . . . Grayshott looks like a doll's village, not so much because of the size of the houses, but because of their quaintness. The upper storeys are covered with lozenge shaped bright red tiles, made at Haslemere. It has a temporary look, and there is the feeling that one could upset it like a village built with a pack of cards. The tiles, which the damp south-west winds render necessary, are secured to walls built not of brick but of wood covered with felt. The houses are all new, having been erected during the last five or six years. Numbers of persons of distinction reside or have resided at or near Hind Head—famous poets, scientists, journalists, painters."

1. The Fox and Pelican refreshment house, where Flora sometimes bought her lunches while working at the Post Office.

Most of the Grayshott people had moved from elsewhere—including distant places such as Birmingham and Shropshire—and had no local roots, which Flora felt affected their character and behaviour, as they tended to live "for the passing moment", and were far more independent and casual in their attitudes than traditional village shopkeepers, and they took less pride in their work.

One place Flora would have known was a curious 'refreshment house' set up in 1899 by the Grayshott and District Refreshment Association as an alternative to a public house, entitled the *Fox and Pelican* after Bishop Fox of Winchester, founder of Corpus Christi College, Oxford, whose device was a 'pelican in her piety', feeding her young with the blood from her own breast. The signboard was painted by Walter Crane. The aim was to discourage drunkenness by providing food, tea and coffee, non-alcoholic drinks and light beers, keeping the stronger alcohol out of sight, to be dispensed on request. It was also a place for people to enjoy their leisure and George Bernard Shaw donated a collection of books for a library there.

Working in the Post Office of such a place was a fascinating adventure for Flora, because she came across a wide variety of people. To her delight several prominent authors were among her customers, and she delighted in listening to their conversation and longed to share in it:

"She would sometimes wish that one of those quick, clever remarks they tossed like coloured glass balls into the air could have come her way, for in her youthful vanity she persuaded herself that she could have caught and returned it more neatly than someone to whom it was addressed."

Heatherley, p. 172

Among the authors she met in this way were George Bernard Shaw, who had just had a cycling accident, " a tall man on a crutch, with a forked red beard and quick, searching eyes, surrounded by a group of young men who appeared to be drinking in his every syllable" and Sir Arthur Conan Doyle, an enormously popular man, who in addition to his Sherlock Holmes novels wrote *Sir Nigel*, a medieval romance published in 1910, based on the local area, especially Frensham, Tilford and Waverley Abbey which Flora probably knew. Another author was Grant Allen who had written a scandalous novel, *The Woman Who Did*, which actually dared to mention sexual problems. Flora commented that it was in fact a serious and literary book, which attracted notoriety because "of its supposed loose morals" and that the scandal made all the locals eager to read it.

Flora also mentions a poet, who "raced about the parish . . . on his bicycle with his halo of long fair hair uncovered and his almost feminine slightness and grace set off by a white silk shirt, big artist's bow tie and velvet knickerbockers", who was Richard le Galliene. She would also have met Henry James, who in 1898 wrote a story about a postmistress, entitled *In the Cage*.

Flora became friendly with various local characters such as broom squires, who earned their living making besoms, and 'Mr Foreshaw', an elderly gentleman who had been a big-game hunter in Africa, and brother and sister 'Richard and Mavis Brownlow', visitors to the area who encouraged Flora to try to take Civil Service exams, which she found too advanced for her and abandoned. The 'Brownlows' were bitterly disappointed at this as they had hoped she would come and work in London, where they lived when she passed them. Flora and Richard grew close, but he confessed to her that he would never be able to afford to marry her.

She also took advantage of her leisure time to explore the countryside around her and the picturesque Waggoner's Wells on the edge of the village became a favourite haunt:

"These three lakes lie along the bottom of a narrow valley, acres of wild heath and woodland surround them on either side; immemorial forest trees line the banks and overhang the still green water, every leaf and twig reflected as in a mirror, so perfect is the image embosomed there that it reminds one irresistibly of the old fabulous drowned forests of legend."

Guide to Liphook, Bramshott and Neighbourhood.

The ponds may have originated as hammer ponds or fishponds created in the seventeenth century by the Hooke family, (who were clothiers until Henry Hooke built an iron mill), by damming a stream which formed part of the headwater of the River Wey. The site was purchased by the National Trust in 1919 as a memorial to Sir Robert Hunter, a founder member. They were originally known as Wakeners Wells.

The Post Office

The Post Office was, like the surrounding buildings, red tiled and Flora wrote that the shop window contained a display of attractive leather goods such as writing cases, purses and photograph frames, plus Bibles and prayer books. It also sold postcards of local views, which cunningly compared the area to the Swiss Alps to attract more visitors. Flora's responsibility was to look after the Post Office for Walter Chapman, who was busy with his work as a cabinet maker, joiner and carpenter, running the Post Office and stationers as a sideline.

She worked with an eighteen year old girl, Annie Symonds, (called Alma Steadman in *Heatherley*), a cheerful girl who soon became a friend. She dealt with postal matters and the telegraph machine, which she taught Annie to use, and prepared the accounts for Walter Chapman to sign.

In *Heatherley* Flora renamed the Chapman family as the Hertfords. Life was not altogether easy for her in Grayshott because she lived in the Chapmans' house, and soon realised that they were very unhappily married. Walter Gilman Chapman was a dark rather wild-eyed man, the son of an innkeeper. He had fallen in love with a local girl but her parents had not approved of the match so he went to Australia to make his fortune. He planned to come back and marry her, but she died just before his return; he never recovered from his grief at her loss. He spent the next years drifting between England and Australia, and it was not until about twenty years later that he met his wife Emily, who was working as a governess to a family visiting the neighbourhood, and they began to go out together. Their behaviour occasioned gossip and she was sacked from her post, upon which he offered to marry her, although admitting that he did not love her. When Flora came to Grayshott he was aged about 45. He clearly enjoyed his cabinet making, specialising in making up furniture to his customers' individual designs, and undertaking major commissions such as the woodwork for a private Catholic chapel.

His wife Emily, aged 37, tall, thin and pale, with a love of music, was heavily pregnant when Flora arrived. The relationship between the couple was strained, with frequent rows. Flora felt like a pig in the middle, particularly when they refused to talk to each other and communicated through her. Walter Chapman was deranged, believing there were intruders in the house at night:

"As far as Laura was concerned, things came to a climax one night after she had gone to bed and heard a loud bang which she thought at first was some kind of explosion. Rushing out on to the landing she found Mrs Hertford, in her nightdress, coaxing her husband back to bed. He held a small revolver in his hand and Mrs Hertford afterwards told Laura that he had thought he heard whispering beneath the landing window, and thinking it was burglars, he had fired his revolver to scare them away. Whether or not the shot scared anyone below, it certainly scared Laura, and she was not at all reassured when, thinking the

2. The Post Office where Flora worked has been demolished, to be replaced by the hip-roofed shops.

proper time had come to tell Mrs Hertford about the footsteps she thought she had heard at night and of her impression that someone had been in her room, she was told that it was one of Mr Hertford's habits to prowl about the house at all hours of the night, opening and shutting doors and looking into dark corners with the idea of finding some unnamed enemy he believed was lying in wait for him. He had sometimes been in Laura's room for it was one of his ideas that Laura might be in league with the enemy. When he had this idea he would call his wife up from her sleep to play propriety, and while she stood at the door, he, with a shaded candle in his hand, would creep softly into the room to see if anyone beside Laura was there. Laura, of course, was always alone and in bed with her hair screwed up in Hind's curlers and her face thickly cold-creamed, and so obviously asleep that, for a time, he was pacified."

Heatherley, pp. 232–3

Flora decided she must find a room in the village, and promised Mrs Chapman faithfully that she would say nothing of her husband's strange behaviour. Not long after, a new telegraph office opened nearby, and there was far less work for Flora. In Spring 1901 she went off to find work elsewhere.

Emily Chapman, again pregnant, left home with her four children to stay with her brother-in-law Ernest Chapman, a Grayshott builder, frightened by her husband's accusations of infidelity and his violence. Just before the baby was due she was persuaded to go back home by Walter, but he soon resumed his accusations. Emily was terrified and confided her fears to the local doctor when the baby was born in June, but he considered Walter not seriously enough deluded to be certifiable.

However on the morning of 29 July 1901 Annie Symonds and Edith Henrietta Smith, working in the Post Office and Gilbert Winchester, Walter's assistant in the workshop, heard screams from the house. Ernest Chapman's evidence at the inquest was reported in the Herald revealed the tragedy that had occurred:

"Witness was going to the office on Monday morning last, and was just getting off his bicycle when Gilbert Winchester beckoned to him, and told him something. The time was about a quarter to ten. Witness rushed into the sitting-room of the deceased and there he saw the deceased lying by the corner of the table, huddled up. He saw no blood at first, but he went to her, knelt down on the floor, and took her up in his arms, and then he noticed a small pool of blood on the floor. The deceased was not dead then, for she groaned a few times. she was not able to speak, for witness spoke to her and she made no reply. He saw no knife or anything like that about then. Witness subsequently saw his brother, who was upstairs, when some little time later he was brought down by the constable..."

The doctor attested that Emily had been stabbed several times in the chest by a sharp instrument, the shank of which was found embedded four inches in the body.

The trial at the Assizes lasted less than two hours and Walter was adjudged guilty but not responsible for his behaviour due to insanity, and he was sentenced to be detained during His Majesty's pleasure.

11

Bournemouth: Married Life

%a

Perhaps her experience at Grayshott deterred Flora from getting another permanent job for a while, or perhaps such jobs were difficult to find. Whatever the reason, Flora's movements for the next two years are uncertain. It was during that time that she met and fell in love with John Thompson, whom she married at the church of St Mary the Virgin in Twickenham, London, presumably near where she was living at the time, on 7 January 1903. None of her family were present—Edwin was serving in the army in India, and it would have been a long and expensive journey from Juniper Hill for Albert and Emma Timms.

John Thompson, who was two years older than Flora, being born on 4 April 1874, came from a very different background. His father Henry Thompson had served as Chief Petty Officer in the Royal Navy. John was one of ten children, brought up in Ryde on the Isle of Wight.

After their marriage Flora and John moved into rented accommodation at number 4 Sedgley Road in Winton, (they later moved to number 6), a village in the parish of Moordown then on the outskirts of Bournemouth, which has since become a suburb. John too worked in the Post Office, and he was at that time a sorting clerk and telegraphist at the main post office in Bournemouth in Beckford Road. Flora, as a married woman, was not permitted to work.

Fortunately she again lived near the countryside, as Winton, like Juniper Hill, had been established on open heathland which was enclosed in 1802. The name was taken from the surname of Winton (a contraction of the Latin name for Winchester) assumed by the Bishop of Winchester, as the area was said to be particularly popular with the bishops. In 1875 Winton was considered big enough to have its own Post Office which opened on the corner of Post Office Road (Castle Road) and Wimborne Road, in the front room of a brick cottage, which was later enlarged to make a double-fronted shop for George Troke's bakery and grocer's shop and Post Office, and a wall letter box was installed. In the 1880s Winton had a population of over 1400, and it was growing rapidly when Flora and John arrived there in 1903.

In 1890, thirteen years before Flora and John came to live there, Winton was thus described in the Parish Magazine:

"Perhaps there is no other such place in the world as Winton, in all events it would be difficult to find one. Some it its characteristics it may no longer retain. We mean the beauty of its golden flowers in May and its purple heather in August. Much of this wild natural beauty has already succumbed. But picturesque as are the gorse and the heather and beautiful as are the glimpses of the Stour Valley, with St Catherine's Hill in the distance and grateful is the shade of the Winton Pines in the summer and their shelter in winter, it must be confessed that Winton's unique attraction consists not in these natural beauties which have their counterparts elsewhere, but in the affable style, disposition and arrangements of the working people's houses, such as in the newer parts of the settlement. It would be difficult to find any other place where so much care has been taken to study from a business point of view the precise wants and wishes of our working people as regards their homes. The houses of the great majority of our working people are not usually very attractive. . . .

Winton is neither country nor town but seems to take practical hints from both. Trees are not favourable to the growth of vegetables and so far the picturesque is a sacrifice to the useful, but the houses themselves are certainly not without their attractiveness nor is the general view of Peters Hill looking south otherwise than picturesque. In the way of improvement there is of course a great deal to be done. The high road requires to be levelled, there is no public form of any kind of entertainment, no proper cricket ground, the supply of drinking water terminates as though Peters Hill was too much for it. The drainage is still primitive, the lighting though admirable depends on voluntary enterprise—a local committee supplies oil lamps etc. The fire engine like the water cart is conspicuous by its absence. Lastly we are, it is supposed, so orderly that we only require, or at least only get, the services of one resident policeman."

Quoted in S.J.Lands, *The Growth of Winton*, Dorset County Council 1970

Wimborne Road, close to the various houses where the Thompsons lived during their time in Winton, had many purpose-built shops, and they had other shops nearby in Talbot Village Road. There was such a wealth of choice that it must have been like living in a small town.

For the first few months Flora delighted in taking long walks to explore the area around her new home. She lived on the edge of Winton, so it did not take long to get to the countryside. One of her favourite walks was to Talbot Village, a model village established in the mid nineteenth century not far from Winton by Miss Georgina Talbot who is described on her memorial cross in St Mark's Church in the village:

"She came of an ancient race, and possessed in herself that nobility of mind which delighted in the happiness of her fellow creatures . . . In the neighbourhood of the village she passed 25 years of a blameless life, giving up time and fortune to bettering the condition of the poorer classes, seeking to minister to their temporal and spiritual welfare, and erecting habitations suitable to their position in life, herself enjoying a peaceful and happy existence in doing good, awaiting the end."

Quoted in Chas. H. Mate and Chas. Riddle, *Bournemouth 1810–1910*, (1910)

Talbot Village had nineteen Gothic cottages each with an acre of garden, even a church and school. The inhabitants had to conform to strict rules of behaviour, the compensation being better accommodation than normally available.

Flora was always interested in literary associations, and another walk she took was to Skerryvore, where Robert Louis Stevenson lived from April 1885 until 1887. The house was given to Mrs Stevenson by her father-in-law. It was renamed 'Skerryvore' after the lighthouse the family firm had built off the Argyll coast. Despite his illness. Stevenson continued to work, and several of his most famous books were written there. He left Bourne-mouth to holiday abroad in August 1887, never to return. However his house was remembered. Flora wrote of it years later:

"Skerryvore stands just as he left it. Memorial tablets to his pet dogs bear witness to his love for all living creatures. In their season rhododendron blooms make vivid splashes of colour against the dark pines that once delighted his artist soul. From the upper windows may still be seen the glimpse of the sea that he delighted to point out to his guests. Only he, the life and soul of it all, has gone."

The Catholic Fireside, 5 June 1920, vol XVIII, no. 1594

Skerryvore was damaged in an air raid in 1940 and subsequently demolished; it was replaced by a memorial garden.

Flora and John's first child, Winifred Grace, was born in the autumn of 1903. She was christened on 7 August 1904 in St John's Church in Moordown. Later in life Winifred preferred to be called Diana. Although Flora could no longer take long solitary walks, with a small baby in tow, and her life must have changed drastically, she continued to read as much as she possibly could, buying cheap second-hand books when she could afford them. She must have been delighted when a new public lending library opened in Winton in 1907. At this time she was not actively writing, but must have been storing up ideas and memories for future use.

Henry Basil Thompson was born on 6 October 1909. That year the family, still in rented accommodation, moved a couple of streets away to 2 Edgehill Road, calling their new home Grayshott Cottage. They had a convenient and comfortable house with a garden, but in some ways Flora seems to have missed the cottage of her childhood with its rag rugs. She still considered herself an onlooker on society, not making many close friends.

It was in 1910 that Flora felt ready to begin writing. She began buying the *Ladies Companion*, attracted by its book club which encouraged readers to read both the classics and good modern English literature. She was fascinated by the literary competitions they ran, and resolved to try her hand at them. The first one Flora entered was in February 1911, on Jane Austen, one of her favourite authors. She must have been astounded when she won the prize - any book of her choice up to the cost of five shillings, and the joy of seeing most of her essay in print:

"Before Jane Austen began to write, the novelists of her day had depended on involved plots, sensational incident, and the long arm of coincidence; therefore when these quiet, gentle stories appeared, dealing with everyday people and events, the public did not immediately recognise her genius or appreciate the gentle sarcasm that plays around her characters. It is true that her genius was at once recognised by a few of the greatest men and women of her time. Sir Walter Scott

1. Flora with her son Basil.

admired her work exceedingly, so did Sydney Smith, the Countess of Morley and, strange to say, the Prince Regent. She found herself, indeed, her own public of devoted admirers, but was then as now 'caviare to the general', ... Jane Austen compared herself to a painter on ivory, and the enjoyment of her work is something like the possession of an exquisite miniature. Those who appreciate her art consider no praise too high. Those who do not, simply wonder how anyone can wade through the dull, tame pages, for no one loves Jane Austen moderately."

The Ladies Companion, February 1911

Flora's writing career had begun gloriously, winning her first competition. Her essay shows that she had done her research thoroughly and methodically, reading as much around the subject as she could. She carried on entering the competitions, winning joint second prize in April for an essay on Emily Brontë and had a mention for her writing on Catherine of Aragon at the end of April, winning again in July on the topic of Shakespeare's Juliet, and her successes continued.

That spring she took her two children for a trip on the train to the New Forest, while John was away at a conference of the United Kingdom Postal Clerks' Association. She loved the area, and when she came to write her nature essays for the *Catholic Fireside*, the first twelve were set in the New Forest, with her usual perceptive comment, such as the importance of forest rights to the commoner who relied on such ancestral rights as digging turf and collecting fallen branches to augment his meagre income.

Flora must have made many visits to the New Forest while she lived at Bournemouth to acquire the material for these articles. She also used the New Forest setting for the first short story she had published, *The Toft Cup*, about the discovery of a valuable cup which saved an old lady from poverty, which appeared in the *Ladies Companion* in January 1912, and in an unpublished novel, *Gates of Eden*. Flora was delighted to be earning money for her work, and determined to earn as much as she could to help pay for her children's education.

One competition she entered in 1912 had a pivotal influence on her future life. She commented on an ode written by the poet Dr. Ronald Campbell Macfie on the sinking of the Titanic. Dr Macfie not only wrote to Flora to say how much he appreciated what she had written, but came to see her in Bournemouth. He was a medical doctor who specialised in the treatment of tuberculosis, and he told Flora he had decided not to marry so that he would be able to concentrate on his writing. He greatly encouraged Flora for many years in her writing of poetry, becoming a very close friend; she did not find it easy to make close friendships and valued his very deeply. It was through his influence that she later began the Peverel Society.

The Thompsons moved again in 1915 to 42 Frederica Road in Winton, two streets away from their original home in Sedgley Road, a detached suburban house, built close to its neighbours on either side, with a gabled roof, and decorative tile-hanging between the upper and lower bay windows, reminiscent of Grayshott. Flora later wrote of this house:

> "Some years ago I was living in a house on the outskirts of Bournemouth, one room of which had a French window opening on to a small lawn with a grassy bank running round it. On this bank I planted dozens of clumps of snowdrops, having them brought specially by gipsies from the New Forest, and adding to them year by year. I left the neighbourhood rather hurriedly at midsummer and the snowdrops were forgotten, but mixed with my regrets for my snowdrops the next winter was a certain pleasure in imagining the new tenants' surprise when they found their grassy banks snowed over with the flowers."

> *The Peverel Papers*, p. 35

In 1915 too, the *Ladies Companion* ceased publication, because of the First World War. Flora did not want to lose the money she had been earning, so she wrote articles for newspapers, more short stories and poems.

A little while after Flora heard that her beloved brother Edwin had been killed in action in Belgium, John Thompson decided to apply for a new job as sub-postmaster in Liphook, not far from where Flora had worked at Grayshott. Perhaps he was influenced in his choice by Flora's grief, feeling that the change would help her, and by the knowledge of how much she loved the area. He was given the job, and in August 1916 they moved to Liphook, hence the reference above to having to leave her newly-planted snowdrops.

12

Liphook and Griggs Green:
The Peverel Papers

ℰ

John Thompson was promoted to sub-postmaster when he and Flora moved to Liphook in 1916. Their Post Office was in the main street in the building now used by the Midland Bank. They were provided with a small house called Ruskin House next to the Post Office which was refurbished for them, with new grates in the sitting rooms and a kitchener range in the kitchen. The Thompson family lived there for about ten years until 1926 when they bought their own house at nearby Griggs Green.

Flora grew to know and love Liphook well, and as her writing developed became well enough known locally to be asked to write a guide book which was published in about 1925. This gives a fascinating glimpse of the village as Flora knew it:

"The Hampshire village of Liphook stands upon the London to Portsmouth road at the junction of three counties, Hampshire, Surrey, and Sussex; 44 miles from London on the one hand and 25 from Portsmouth on the other . . .

Lying upon the borders of three of the most beautiful counties in the South of England the district around Liphook combines within itself the attractions of the whole three. The moorland pine and heather of Hampshire; the leafy vales, deep lanes and sparkling water-courses of Surrey; the turf and thyme-scented chalk downs of Sussex, all are within easy reach by foot, cycle or car . . .

In the heart of this lovely country, the white walls of its principal buildings tree-embowered, its roads wide and clean, its gardens bright with flowers and pleasant with healthy faces, at a point where six roads meet and form the "loop" from which it was probably named, stands the village of Liphook.

Technically speaking, it is not a village at all, but a hamlet of the neighbouring, but much smaller village of Bramshott."

Guide to Liphook, Bramshott and Neighbourhood

Flora went on to describe the village square dominated by the Anchor Inn, an old coaching house with a Georgian facade, where such illustrious people as Samuel Pepys and Smollet had stayed. It could even boast of receiving royalty, as in 1815 the Prince Regent entertained the allied sovereigns there to celebrate victory at the Battle of Waterloo, and later the young Princess Victoria had bowed to the crowds from an upper window.

Perhaps she was reminded of distant Fringford when she wrote of the old smithy on the opposite side of the square:

"The smithy is very ancient, as the outside appearance testifies, but, even so, it must have been built to replace an even earlier one, for antique documents mention a forge of some kind upon the site as early as the beginning of the fifteenth century.

Probably the days of the present one are numbered, for, after being in the occupation of one family for two centuries the ashes are cold, the anvil silent. A large and prosperous motor garage a few yards farther on provides for the different needs of the twentieth-century traveller by the Portsmouth road."

Guide to Liphook, Bramshott and Neighbourhood

She goes on to describe the other parts of the hamlet, including the elms and beeches of Chitley Park and the ancient Ship Inn which made up the old part, and the newer villas of Headley Road, the Newtown area of shops and houses, even a golf course, adding to the amenities:

"The social life of the place is very pleasant. Between twenty and thirty large country houses and estates, many of them of great beauty and interest, lie within the postal delivery . . . For the village there is a Tennis Club with well-appointed courts, Cricket and Football Clubs, the latter of more than local repute: a Village Hall where dances are held and concert and theatrical companies give constantly changing performances: the Boy Scout and Girl Guide movements are especially flourishing, while the Women's Institute, there as elsewhere, has worked wonders in brightening village life.

Enough it is hoped, has been said to prove that at Liphook may be found fine air and natural beauty in fullest measure without the least sacrifice of personal comfort; peace and quiet without stagnation; and that it is no mushroom pleasure place sprung up in a few months to batten upon the health or pleasure seeker, but an old English village, a centre, small but exquisite, where the art of entertaining is hereditary."

Guide to Liphook, Bramshott and Neighbourhood

It is evident from her guidebook how much she loved the area, and how well she grew to know all the best walks, finding her own favourite spots such as Weaver's Down:

"Gilbert White describes Weaver's Down as "A vast hill on the eastern side of Woolmer", and although the "vastness" of it fails to impress modern eyes, its wild and rugged beauty is unaltered. It is a land of warm sands, of pine and heather and low-lying boglands; a stretching moor through which the spur of the South Downs, terminating in the little rounded hill, rising like a miniature mountain upon the Liphook side, runs like a back-bone.

From the summit upon a clear day a magnificent view rewards the climber: Heath and woodland, green field and glinting stream lie stretched at his feet, a perfect panorama of beauty. Forestmere Lake lies like a mirror in the woods directly beneath; to the south is the blue ridge of the South Downs; to the north the heathery heights of Hindhead."

Guide to Liphook, Bramshott and Neighbourhood

The guide is full of advertisements which indicate the varied commercial aspect of Liphook, such as hotels, (the Railway Hotel offered: "Good accommodation for Golfing, Cyclists, Touring and Char-a-banc Parties. Moderate terms on application to the Proprietor, E. W. Bosley. Within easy distance of the fine Liphook Golf Links. Motors and Carriages at most Moderate Charges . . ."), builders, surveyors and undertakers, a garage, blacksmith and printers. There was a wide variety of shops including two clock and watchmakers and jewellers, a boot and shoe maker and an upholsterer. Stationery and ironmongery were available from The People's Stores in the Square, while H. Budd who sold beekeepers' supplies was also a carpenter, painter and house decorator.

Many shops sold food: including various 'provision merchants' and even department stores including the General Supply Stores who claimed to be "the leading dry goods store in the district, departments include ladies' and childrens' outfitting, millinery, hosiery and boots, furniture (new and second-hand and antique), beds and bedding, hardware, china, soaps and polishes".

Miss A.B.Skevington was head teacher of the Day School for Girls and Preparatory School for Boys in Liphook where she offered: 'Sound education on modern lines. Pupils prepared for Public Examination if desired. The curriculum includes all ordinary subjects, and Latin, French, Drawing, Nature Study, Class Singing, Handwork and Needlework. Visiting Mistresses for Games, Music and Dancing. Private Lessons in Literature, French and Latin by arrangement.'

Despite being described as a hamlet, it was a far cry from Juniper Hill which could only boast the little shop in the back room of the inn.

The Thompsons moved to Liphook at a difficult time, as Flora was grieving after the death of her beloved brother Edwin and war brought extra duties for both John and herself in the Post Office. It was fortunate that they lived next door so that the post could be brought in to Flora at

1. The site of the Post Office run by John Thompson in Liphook, now replaced by the Midland Bank.

4a.m. each morning for sorting, while Winifred and Basil were still asleep, and for Clara Louise Woods to collect at 5.45 ready to cycle the twenty mile delivery round, which she did twice a day. John had to spend many nights sleeping on an uncomfortable camp bed in the post office in case telegrams came through. It is ironic that much mail was for Canadian soldiers stationed at nearby Bramshott, which must have reminded Flora constantly of the death of Edwin, who had been in the Canadian army.

Despite the arduous post office work, the household chores and task of bringing up her family, Flora managed to snatch time to write in her own haven—a little room, sparsely furnished with her desk, chair and waste-paper basket, where she could read and write in peace. Then, to her surprise and perhaps initial dismay, she found herself pregnant again at 40. Once her beloved son Peter Redmond was born money was tight; they had not anticipated any more children so all the baby equipment had to be bought again. Time, too, was at a premium with three children.

After the war Flora was released from the chore of sorting the mail and Winifred and Basil were at school so she was able to continue her personal development, improving her writing by becoming a student on a postal course run by the Practical Correspondence College in London. It was probably through this that Flora began writing for the *Catholic Fireside*, which was to be influential in her career, giving her the scope to write about the nature she loved so much; she gradually began to incorporate into her articles the memories of her childhood which were to develop into *Lark Rise to Candleford*. The first writing she had published in the *Catholic Fireside*, in 1921, was a rewritten romantic story with a medieval theme entitled *The Leper*, then she began her series of nature articles in 1921.

Flora gave herself a new persona as author of these pieces, explaining to her readers that she was a doctor's daughter who lived in a little cottage in the New Forest, perhaps because she felt her real background would make her seem inferior to her middle-class readers.

Flora at this time achieved local fame in Liphook when her slim volume of poetry, *Bog Myrtle and Peat*, was published in 1921. The *Daily Chronicle* of 2 March 1921 described her in a headline as "Woman of Letters. Village Postmistress Poetess—Her First Volume", going on to say:

"The people of Liphook have always believed that the pleasant situation of their village, and the natural beauties of their countryside, they had enough for proper local pride. Now they find that they possess a hitherto undiscovered and unsuspected poetess."

One can imagine Flora's embarrassment at reading this, as she was still a very shy, private person, but it caused great amusement in the family. In her heart of hearts, Flora longed to be a good poet, but although *Bog Myrtle and Peat* was well reviewed it did not sell very well, and the quality of her poetry did not match that of her prose.

In 1922 the character of her writing for the *Catholic Fireside* changed, to concentrate on nature, and her middle-class persona was no longer used. Her essays were retitled *The Peverel Papers*—no-one has definitively explained how she chose the name. She continued the series for six years. Most of her writing was based on the walks she enjoyed around Weaver's Down, Waggoner's Wells and Wheatsheaf Common. Flora liked to incorporate historical anecdotes into her writing, such as this one, about Woolmer Forest, close to which she later lived:

> "At noon I rested upon a smooth mound, still known as Queen's Bank, though few remember it as the spot where Queen Anne, turning aside from the main road on her way seaward, condescended to rest and behold the magnificent herd of five hundred red deer, which were rounded up and driven through the valley for the pleasure of their royal owner.
>
> The forest was old in Queen Anne's Day. Along the valley she overlooked from her bank the young Black Prince must often have passed with his hawk and hounds in the days when his parents had a hunting lodge close by. And even that older Woolmer was but a section cut from the still older forest of Andredswold, which stretched, a great wold-infested wilderness, from the borders of Kent to the Hampshire Downs.
>
> There are no red deer in Woolmer to-day. The fine herd of five hundred had dwindled to fifty by the middle of the eighteenth century, and these were eventually captured and carried in carts to Windsor."
>
> *The Peverel Papers*, p. 175

Flora's deep love for and sensitive observation of the area is shown in this description of one of her favourite haunts, the Hermit's pool:

> "In the woods by the Hermit's pool this glamorous quiet is especially noticeable. Scarce a leaf stirs or a wavelet ripples; the air is warm and heavy with the dank colours of tree-bark, moss and waterweeds. Over the long vistas of the narrow pathways a light fleece of greyish-purple

mist floats until midday, even when the sky above the tree-tops is gold-shot with sunshine and the heath outside crackling dry with heat. The beeches upon the shore of the lake are already in their full October glory of gold and russet and amber, every leaf and twig so faithfully reflected in the still waters that it seems that a second beechwood is submerged there, like one of the old drowned forests of legend."

The Peverel Papers, p. 180

Peverel had another significance for Flora. Once Peter started school in 1923 she found she had some additional time, and suggested to the *Catholic Fireside* that she start The Fireside Reading Circle, for which she wrote well researched literary essays, and organised writing competitions. Through this she became friendly with Mildred Humble-Smith, who entered the competitions. Mildred was the daughter of a ship's chandler and nautical instrument maker from Newcastle on Tyne, and like Flora was married, and had two sons. She had studied English in Oxford, although as Oxford did not confer degrees on women at that time her degrees were nominally from Edinburgh and Durham. Her husband had left the Brazilian navy and the family settled in Wimborne, Dorset, so she and Flora were able to meet, and as they became close friends they formed the Peverel Society together and she ended the Fireside Reading Circle in November 1925.

The annual subscrtiption of their new circle, The Peverel Society, which catered for poets and prose writers was seven shillings and sixpence. A brochure for the society, written later when she was living in Dartmouth, described how it operated: saying that it was formed "for the mutual pleasure and advantage of writers, and those learning to write for the press". The members would each submit a story, article or poem to the Secretary by the beginning of each month. The Secretary divided these into groups according to individual requirements and made up a portfolio for each group. These were circulated from one member of the group to the next, each one writing comments on the work before sending it on. The aim was for each member to get a variety of sympathetic comments on the work sent in. A 'Chats Book' was included with the portfolio, giving ideas on how to find the right markets for the work, discussing literary topics and answering queries. Flora hoped that in this way the writers would form friendships.

Membership built up to over a hundred people from all over Britain, some being established writers, others novices. The brochure ended: "A HEARTY WELCOME AND THE HELPING HAND OF FRIENDLY CRITICISM AWAITS YOU!"

It was while she was at Liphook that Flora found another avenue for her talents, answering an advertisement in a literary journal for a ghost writer to a big game hunter, and writing articles for him which appeared in *Chamber's Journal*, the *Scottish Field* and various African papers. The influence of this can be seen in some of her writing in *Lark Rise*, particularly the pig-killing scene:

"The killing was a noisy, bloody business, in the course of which the animal was hoisted to a rough bench that it might bleed thoroughly and so preserve the quality of the meat. The job was often bungled, the pig sometimes getting away and having to be chased; but country people of that day had little sympathy for the suffering of animals, and men, women and children would gather round to see the sight.

After the carcass had been singed, the pig-sticker would pull off the detachable, gristly, outer coverings of the toes, known locally as 'the shoes', and fling them among the children, who scrambled for, then sucked and gnawed them, straight from the filth of the sty and blackened by fire as they were.

The whole scene, with its mud and blood, flaring lights and dark shadows, was a savage as anything to be seen in an African jungle ...

But, hidden from the children, there was another aspect of the pig-killing. Months of hard work and self-denial were brought on that night to a successful conclusion. It was a time to rejoice, and rejoice they did, with beer flowing freely and the first delicious dish of pig's fry sizzling in the frying-pan."

Lark Rise to Candleford, p. 26

As well as the reference to the African jungle, this quotation illustrates another important aspect of Flora's work—it would have been easy to have seen the late Victorian era, as many writers have done, in a rosy glow, but all the way through *Lark Rise to Candleford* are little asides like the one above, which show Flora's clear understanding of the arduous aspects of life endured by the villagers.

Flora is commemorated in Liphook by a charming memorial sculpture, created by Philip Jackson, and presented by the Bramshott and Liphook Preservation Society. It is taken from the wistful photograph of Flora as a young woman, and evocatively portrays her shy, rather diffident character. It is now housed in the library as it was sadly vandalised when left outside. The original statue was unveiled in 1981 and a renovated version put in the library in 1995.

2. The statue of Flora Thompson by Philip Jackson, commissioned by the Bramshott and Liphook Preservation Society, housed in Liphook Library.

Griggs Green

In 1926 a night-time switchboard operator was appointed by the Post Office to help John, which made it easier for him to live further away from work. The Thompsons decided to buy a house of their own, instead of living in Post Office accommodation. Through Flora's influence they found a house at Grigg's Green, a place she already knew well and had grown to love from her walks:

> "The older portion of the hamlet of Griggs Green, (one mile from the Square) consists chiefly of a smithy, an inn, and a row of white-washed

cottages standing back from the road upon a tree-shaded green. The inn, The Deer's Hut, was, as its name implies, one of the old forest ale-houses, nor has its function altered much, for neighbours from the scattered houses upon the heath still meet there upon summer evenings to take their glass and discuss things upon the green before the door, just as their forebears must have done for centuries.

To reach Weaver's Down, leave the Longmoor Road at the Deer's Hut, and take the footpath which passes its doorway. Just a fringe is left there of the old primeval forest oak and holly and immemorial yew, but very soon this is left behind and the open heath of which Woolmer at this day chiefly consists lies spread before the wayfarer.... the geologist, naturalist or beauty-lover will each find a happy hunting ground there, and one that has scarcely been touched since Gilbert White wrote of it."

Guide to Liphook, Bramshott and Neighbourhood

Flora called her house in Longmoor Road Woolmer Cottage (it has now been renamed Woolmer Gate). It was a comfortable little red tiled cottage, rural in feel, with pine trees behind. She delighted in the peaceful surroundings and easy access along the sandy paths to her beloved Weaver's Down, where she was often accompanied by her now grown-up daughter Winifred. She was working split shifts from nine in the morning until one and again from four thirty in the afternoon until eight, operating the Post Office telephone exchange.

The Thompsons were fortunate in their neighbours, the Leggett family, who lived at Grove House. They often let Peter visit them at the farm, which he loved, and which gave Flora peace and quiet to write.

At this time one of Flora's sisters, Betty, who was also a writer, often came to stay. She had a book published long before Flora, a story about gnomes on Dartmoor, written for children and entitled *The Little Grey Men of the Moor*. Flora must have been enormously proud of her sister's achievements, and perhaps it encouraged her to think more of writing books herself.

Having settled so comfortably in their own home, in such perfect surroundings, it was a cruel shock for Flora when John announced that he had been offered the job of Postmaster in Dartmouth in Devon; which he had applied for secretly, without consulting her. It was a good career move for him, offering promotion, perhaps his last chance of it, as he was then 53, but for Flora it was a bitter blow. Fortunately she had a stay of execution, as

John was unable to find anywhere suitable for them to live straightaway, so she, Winifred and Peter were able to stay at Woolmer Cottage for almost a year longer.

The move saw the end of her Peverel Paper series, the last one being published in December 1927. Eventually the move was organised and the day that Flora left there was torrential rain all day, echoing her sadness at leaving. The rain gave the house and grounds a desolate feel, with the rain dripping from the trees, and there was scarcely even time to visit the grave of a beloved dog in the garden because the taxi was waiting to take them to the railway station for their long journey down to Devon and their new life.

13

Dartmouth and Brixham:
Lark Rise is Born

Flora was devastated to leave the house in Griggs Green that she had loved so much to come to Devon, where she spent the rest of her life, but she gradually grew to enjoy the area. John, having been brought up on the Isle of Wight, was delighted to be near the sea again, and soon bought himself a little motor boat, the *Sea Mew*, in which he and Peter went fishing.

Their new house, called The Outlook, was on the hillside above the main part of the town in an area called Above Town. It was so steep that the house had to be reached by some steps, making furniture removal hard work. The area was criss-crossed with little alleys and from the house there were wonderful views towards Kingswear, the town of Dartmouth itself, and the estuary leading down to the sea. John built Flora a special room where she could write in the garden.

The Dartmouth area had been settled since Saxon times and has a rich legacy of history, greatly influenced by its natural harbour. The Normans used it as their main base in the area; William Rufus, hearing that his town of Le Mans was under siege while he was hunting on Dartmoor, sailed to the rescue from Dartmouth in 1099, and seven ships set off to the Third Crusade from here in 1190. Geoffrey Chaucer visited the town, and his Shipman in the Prologue of the *Canterbury Tales* is said to have been the local merchant John Hawley.

The town was protected by a castle and Edward IV decreed that the haven should be protected by a chain across it. In the sixteenth century the Crescent from Dartmouth engaged Spanish ships off Start Point during the campaign against the Spanish Armada.

Trade was also important, fish, wine and tin being two major commodities. It was from here that the explorer Sir Humphrey Gilbert set out on voyages of discovery in 1578 and again in 1583, with Sir Walter Raleigh, on the latter occasion discovering Newfoundland. It was from here too that the first journey of the East India Company set out in 1601.

As it had such a close association with the sea it is hardly surprising that ship-building flourished here at Sandquay from the early 19th century. It was at Sandquay that Philip and Son, the ship builders who later employed Flora's son Peter, set up in 1858. A further indication of the town's important links with the sea was the opening in 1905 of the Britannia Royal Naval College in Dartmouth.

Flora's interest was more in the countryside around her than the history of the town, and she soon began to explore her surroundings. She was very fond of the coastal area round St Petrox Church and Castle Cove. St Petrox began life as a small monastery at the mouth of the River Dart, first mentioned in 1192, which seems to have maintained a beacon to guide shipping away from the rocks. The church was rebuilt in 1641, and used to house provisions for the castle during the Civil War. By Flora's time it was only used for occasional services during the summer. The tiny church has dramatic impact, with water coming right up to the walls of the churchyard, which are crenellated like the castle. Castle Cove is named after Dartmouth Castle, which, when it was built between 1481 and 1495 to replace an earlier one built in the late fourteenth century, was highly advanced in style, being the first English castle designed for use with firearms, with rectangular gunports similar to those on contemporary warships covering the area of the Dart estuary. It consists of a cylindrical and a square tower adjacent to each other set on the rocky river bank, facing Kingswear Castle, which is now a private house, on the opposite bank.

Flora and John discovered the delights of Dartmoor together, walking in Wistman's Woods, near Two Bridges, with its ancient wizened oak trees, covered in lichen, now a nature reserve, which must have enchanted her.

Flora continued with her writing, concentrating on short stories and books, most of which were never published, and running the Peverel Society. She was yet to find her real niche. She suffered a great personal blow when her mentor and sympathetic friend Dr Macfie died in 1931, as she had benefitted greatly from his encouragement of her writing. He was one of the few people she could talk to about her writing and he was sorely missed for the rest of her life. In 1944 she wrote to Leslie Castle:

"I am sorry to hear you have lost your friend for I know well what a blank such losses mean, although you may find others afterwards that you like as well it is never in quite the same way. The chief friend of my life was a Scotsman, Doctor Ronald Macfie, and I lost him by death ten years ago, a loss never to be replaced."

It was not until 1935, two years after her mother Emma's death, when she herself was nearly 59, that she began to consider seriously writing about her childhood, making a start by noting down details of some of the rhymes connected with the children's games.

Perhaps stimulated by these thoughts of her childhood, Flora sent off a story entitled *The Tail-less Fox*, which she had written at Liphook, about a poor woman with six children, to the *Lady*, perhaps to test the waters to see whether there was a market for such work. She must have been delighted when it was published in 1936, and capitalised on it by sending off an article on Queenie, the lacemaker she had known in Juniper Hill, which was published in April 1937.

She wrote fourteen more essays about her childhood, narrated by her *alter ego* Laura, and then she plucked up the courage to send them to Oxford University Press, perhaps a strange choice as they had a policy of not publishing fiction. However, Sir Humphrey Milford, the Publisher, was immediately aware of the value of her work, and encouraged her to amplify what she had written into a book, and agreed to publish it as an auto-biography. Flora was such an unassuming person that she would never have written an autobiography in the strict sense, to draw attention to herself, but by making herself the onlooker on the local scene, depicted the places and life around her, using her creative talents to embellish them, and disguise personalities. Geoffrey Cumberlege was her editor, and he became a friend over the years they collaborated over her work. Lynton Lamb was commissioned to visit the Juniper Hill area and make ten pen and ink drawings to illustrate the book.

The Press published *Lark Rise* in March 1939, and Flora must have been delighted to find it favourably reviewed in such prestigious publications as *Country Life*, the *Yorkshire Post*, the *Sunday Times*, the *Times Literary Supplement* and *Time and Tide*. The accolades give great credit to a woman who, despite her background, achieved evocative writing about her own experience which is still popular half a century after her death.

Flora carried on writing, continuing the tale of her childhood with *Over to Candleford*, which expanded on her visits to her relatives in Twyford and Buckingham. However she could not be unaffected by events in the outside world, as Britain drifted inexorably towards war with Germany, which was finally declared in September. The Thompsons were painfully aware of the dangers of their situation in Dartmouth and were fearful for the safety of the children. Winifred was on holiday in Switzerland when war was declared but accomplished the journey home without any problems, and was amazed when she got home to read in the newspapers that other travellers had encountered insults and hindrances. Basil was in Australia with his family, but Peter was drawn into the war, at first working long hours in Philip's shipyard, then joining the Merchant Navy.

Dartmouth was drastically affected by the Second World War. Philip's yard had to be guarded by the army, and during the war converted many boats for naval use. This obviously made the town a prime target for bombs, and the shipyard and the Naval College were both hit in 1942. The naval students were removed to Cheshire. Two years later the College buildings became the headquarters for American forces.

Flora had to abandon her writing for days to make blackout curtains for the house, and both she and John felt vulnerable living in Dartmouth. John had retired from the Post Office in 1935, but was running his own business renting and buying property and became an ARP warden at the beginning of the war.

In March 1940, John and Flora left the town to live a few miles away in Brixham. Their new house, Lauriston, was a cottage positioned end on to the road, again on a hillside, away from the town centre. The house was big enough to let Flora have her own study in a spare room, and a cellar was converted into a Morrison air-raid shelter, which she had to retreat to often, armed with her precious manuscripts, over the next few years. As John was now buying antiques on commission for a local shop, she was able to collect some small pieces to decorate the house. Flora soon started work again and the proofs for *Over to Candleford* were completed by February 1941, although she said that she did not consider it as good as *Lark Rise*. Geoffrey Cumberlege immediately encouraged her to begin the next book.

Life hit her a hard blow that September, however: Peter was lost at sea when his ship, the *Jedmoor*, was torpedoed in the Atlantic. She must have kept a photograph of him displayed in the house because she wrote to Leslie Castle on 27 January 1946:

"I cut one lovely red rose (garden not greenhouse) on Christmas day to stand beside Peter's photograph, so that show how mild the weather has been, really, though to me it has often seemed cold."

Perhaps throwing herself into writing helped to ease the overwhelming grief. This time she abandoned the theme of *Lark Rise* to write *Dashpers*, the story of a house and its various owners, some of which does seem to take her back to her Oxfordshire roots. However Flora became ill, developing pneumonia and was not able to write for a while. When she felt well enough to start again, she deferred further writing on *Dashpers* and started work on *Candleford Green*, the third volume of the trilogy, which described her life once she had moved to Fringford to work in the Post Office.

Despite the privations of the war, Flora was able to have *Candleford Green* ready for publication in January 1943, again receiving wonderful reviews. She was too tired to begin anything new, and had a lukewarm response to her suggestion that she finish *Dashpers* for Oxford University Press. Geoffrey Cumberlege liked the idea of doing something with the *Peverel Papers*, but for some reason nothing came of that then, or for another thirty years.

She was encouraged to hear of plans to publish her three books as a trilogy, *Lark Rise to Candleford*, illustrated with wood engravings by Julie Neild, and introduced by H.J.Massingham, a noted writer on rural topics. He skilfully stressed the importance of the social historical element in her work:

"It is clear, then, that Flora Thompson's simple-seeming chronicles of life in hamlet, village and market town are, when regarded as an index to social change, of great complexity and heavy with revolutionary meaning. But this you do not notice until you look below the surface. The surface is the family lives and characters of Laura and her neighbours at Lark Rise, inhabited by ex-peasants, and the two Candlefords, where society is more mixed and occupations more varied. But the surface is transparent, and there are threatening depths of dislocation and frustration below it. Flora Thompson's method of revealing them is a literary one, as was George Eliot's; that is to day, by the selective representation of domestic interiors in which living personages pass their daily lives. The social document is a by-product of people's normal activities and by intercourse intensely localized, just as beauty is a by-product of the craftsman's utility-work for his neighbours."

The first edition of the trilogy was sold out even before it was published on 12 April 1945, again to great praise. Flora did not rest on her laurels, starting a new book she entitled *These Too Were Victorians*, (later retitled *Still Glides the Stream*) which was again written about Oxfordshire, with her main character Charity, a schoolteacher. In the typescripts she has sometimes muddled the names *Laura* and *Charity*, even on the same page, and it is evident from the book that many of Charity's characteristics are those of Flora herself. Charity is, like Laura, the pivot of the story, which is written in very much the same style as *Lark Rise to Candleford*. Fascinatingly, Flora wrote of Charity that she relished skipping, a characteristic she herself was remembered for in Juniper Hill:

> "She herself had trodden it [the footpath] daily, often with her skipping rope, her white pinafore billowing, her long hair streaming, her feet scarcely touching the ground."
>
> *Still Glides the Stream*, p. 9

Could there also be an echo of her relationship with her students in the Peverel Society, for whom she acted as teacher in her description of Charity and her pupils:

> "Years of hard work and many disappointments, a typical school-marm's life. But there had been compensations. One here and there of her pupils had shown the sudden gleam of comprehension, the mental and spiritual response to her teaching which sometimes in her lighter moments she had referred to when talking to her colleagues as 'plugging in', or 'taking the bait', but which in her secret thoughts she had treasured as her most precious experience. That, and the privilege of fostering such promise, had been the chief joy of her life; but there had also been material advantages, personal independence, a home of her own, books, friends and holiday travel."
>
> *Still Glides the Stream*, p.10

The village of Restharrow in which the book is set is thought to be based on Stoke Lyne or Hethe, both in the same area as *Lark Rise*, but they are less specifically described than Juniper Hill and Cottisford, and few characters are readily identifiable. However a few pieces of the jig-saw can be put together. For example the bungalow mentioned on the first page, which housed the retired village policeman, may have been one of a row of bungalows in Fringford, one of which housed P.C. Manning, who had been the village policeman in Hethe and had also worked for the Metropolitan Police as specified in the book.

It was a much more of a struggle writing this book, because Flora's health was declining, and she suffered from angina, which often confined her to bed, and prevented her from enjoying her walks. However, she finished the book in August 1946. The new title was derived from Wordsworth's *River Dudden*: "Still glides the stream and shall forever glide."

Flora managed to travel to Dartmouth on Armistice Day in November 1946 to lay a wreath of poppies for Peter, and was pleased that her nephew Leslie Castle laid one for Edwin at Cottisford war memorial. Through the cold winter she corrected the proofs of *Still Glides the Stream*. However, in May, when she seemed so much better that John had dared to leave her for a day while he went off on business, Flora had another angina attack, and he came home to find her back in bed. She died peacefully later that evening, before seeing *Still Glides the Stream* in print.

After the funeral service at St Barnabas' church in Dartmouth, she was cremated and her ashes are buried in Longcross Cemetery, Dartmouth. Her gravestone is in the shape of an open book, with "To the dear memory of Flora Thompson May 21st 1947" on the left hand page, and "and of her beloved younger son Peter Redmond Thompson, M.N. lost at sea September 16th 1941" on the right hand page. It is typically unpretentious, giving away little about a very private woman, who yet managed to reveal much of herself and much of the world of her childhood in the pages of her books.

1. The stone commemorating Flora Thompson and her son Peter in Longcross Cemetery, Dartmouth. (William Hunwick)

BIBLIOGRAPHY

BLOMFIELD, J. C., *History of the Present Deanery of Bicester*, published in 8 parts between 1882 and 1894

ENGLISH, BARBARA., Lark Rise *and Juniper Hill: A Victorian Community in Literature and History, Victorian Studies*, volume 29, Autumn 1985

HEMERY, ERIC., *Historic Dart*, David & Charles, 1982

HEDGES, S.G., *Bicester Wuz a Little Town*, Bicester Advertiser, 1968

HORN, PAMELA., *North Oxfordshire Village Life: Flora Thompson and* Lark Rise to Candleford, *Oxfordshire Local History*, Vol 2 No 8, Spring 1986

——*The Juniper Hill Mob*, Limited Edition of the *Oxford Times*, July 1991, no. 57

LANE, MARGARET, *Flora Thompson*, John Murray, 1977

LANDS, S.J., *The Growth of Winton*, Dorset County Council 1970

LINDSAY, GILLIAN, *Flora Thompson, The Story of the* Lark Rise *Writer*, Robert Hale, 1990

Liphook Community Magazine, summer 1981, summer 1985, autumn 1986, autumn 1995

MATE, CHAS. H, and RIDDLE, CHAS, *Bournemouth 1810–1910*, Bournemouth 1910

REED, MICHAEL, *The Buckinghamshire Landscape*, Hodder and Stoughton, 1979

SMITH, J. H., *Grayshott, the Story of a Hampshire Village*, Westwood, 1978

SMITH, John O., *On The Trail of Flora Thompson beyond Candleford Green*, John Owen Smith, 1997

STEANE, JOHN M., *The Northamptonshire Landscape*, Hodder and Stoughton, 1974

THOMPSON, FLORA. *Lark Rise to Candleford*, Penguin 1973

THOMPSON, FLORA. *Still Glides the Stream*, Oxford University Press, 1948

THOMPSON, FLORA (ed. Margaret Lane). *The Country Calendar*, Oxford University Press, 1979

THOMPSON, FLORA, *The Peverel Papers*, Century Hutchinson, 1986

THOMPSON, FLORA, *Guide to Liphook, Bramshott and Neighbourhood*, c1925

TROTTER, W. R., *The Hilltop Writers*, Book Guild, 1996

TUDOR JONES, J. S., *Headley 1066–1966: The Story of a Hampshire Parish*, 1966

YOUNG, DAVID S., *The Story of Bournemouth*, Hale, 1970

ed. WILLIAM PAGE. *Victoria History of the County of Buckingham, vol 4*, London 1927

ed. MARY D. LOBEL. *Victoria History of the County of Oxfordshire, Volume VI, Ploughley Hundred*, Oxford University Press, 1959

WING, WILLIAM. *Brief Annals of the Bicester Poor Law Union and its Component Parishes in the Counties of Oxford and Buckingham*, Bicester 1879

FLORA THOMPSON'S TIMELINE

29.7.1875	Albert Timms, stonemason, and Emma Dibber married and rented a cottage in Juniper Hill.
13.11.1875	Their first daughter, Martha was born, but died two weeks later.
5.12.1876	Flora Jane Timms was born at Juniper Hill. She was baptised in Cottisford Church on 4 March 1877.
2.11.1879	Edwin Timms was baptised.
1882	Flora started school in Cottisford.
4.4.1882	Albert Timms was born—he lived only one day.
3.2.1884	May Timms was baptised.
1.8.1886	Ethel Elizabeth Timms was baptised.
30.3.1887	Emma Timms' father John Dibber was buried at Cottisford Church.
1887	Queen Victoria's Golden Jubilee celebrations were held in Shelswell Park.
1888	Probably the year Flora and Edwin first walked to 'Candleford' (Twyford) on their own to stay with Uncle Tom.
7.10.1888	Frank Wallington Timms was born.
1888	Flora Timms won the Diocesan Prize at school, having been commended in 1886 and 1887.
2.11.1890	Annie Gertrude Timms was baptised.
1891	Flora went to work at Fringford Post Office for Mrs. Whitton.
7.5.1893	Ellen Mary Timms was baptised. She lived only fourteen months, being buried on 26 March 1895.
1897	Flora left Fringford and took a series of temporary post office jobs, in various places, possibly at Twyford, Bucks and including Essex before going to work for Walter Chapman at Grayshott Post Office, Hampshire.
6.3.1898	Cecil Barrie Timms was baptised. He lived to the age of two and a half, being buried on 7.4.1900.
1899	Edwin fought in the Boer War in South Africa. He was captured

by the Boers and abandoned in the Veldt, narrowly escaping dying of thirst. His regiment went straight from South Africa to India after the war, where he stayed for five years.

1901	Flora left Grayshott and did more temporary jobs.
29.7.1901	Walter Chapman murdered his wife Emily.
7.1.1903	Flora Jane Timms married John Thompson at the Church of St Mary the Virgin, Twickenham. None of Flora's family were at the ceremony. John was the son of Emily and Henry Thompson, a Chief Petty Officer in the Royal Navy. The couple went to live in Winton, Bournemouth where John was a sorting clerk and telegraphist at the main Post Office.
1903	Flora and John's daughter Winifred Grace was born. Although busy as a housewife and mother, Flora continued to educate herself by borrowing books from the local library.
1907	Edwin Timms came back from India on leaving the army. He worked on an Oxfordshire farm for two years but, depressed at the low wages, decided to emigrate to Canada.
1909	Flora and Winifred travelled by train to Aynho and pony and trap to Juniper Hill to stay with her family and see Edwin before he left England.
6.10.1909	Flora and John's son Henry Basil was born on 6th October. The family moved to 2 Edgehill Road, Winton, which they renamed Grayshott Cottage (they had previously moved from no. 4 to no. 6 Sedgley Road, Winton).
1910	Flora began to buy *The Ladies Companion* and was about to enter their literary competitions when John succumbed to appendicitis and had to be nursed at home for two weeks.
February 1911	Flora entered a competition in *The Ladies Companion* to write a 300 word essay about Jane Austen, and won the five shilling prize and had most of the essay published.
April 1911	Flora was mentioned in *The Ladies Companion* for her essay on Catherine of Aragon.
Summer 1911	John Thompson's mother died on the Isle of Wight.
January 1912	Flora's first story *The Toft Cup* was published in *The Ladies Companion* and Flora began to realise that she could earn money from her writing. Several more of her stories were published in the magazine over the next couple of years.
1912	Flora first came into contact with Dr Ronald Campbell Macfie, Scottish physician and writer, after entering a competition to com-

ment on his ode on the sinking of the Titanic. He greatly encouraged her writing, particularly her poetry over the next few years.

1913   Flora sold *The Leper* to *The Literary Monthly*.

1914   Flora and John took their family to visit John's widowed father on the Isle of Wight.

1915   *The Ladies Companion* stopped publication. The Thompson's moved to 42 Frederica Road, Winton, which they renamed Grayshott Cottage.
Edwin joined the Eastern Ontario Regiment in Canada. He was given home leave in March, but Flora was unable to visit him because the children had whooping cough, and there was snow. Edwin was posted to France and killed in action. He was buried in Woods cemetery, Zillebeke, Belgium.

1916   John Thompson was promoted to sub-postmaster and the family moved to Liphook to live in Ruskin House adjoining the Post Office (now the Midland Bank). Flora spent four hours from 4am each morning sorting the post from home and John spent many nights sleeping on a camp bed in the post office in case of telegrams.

1918   Flora and John's son Peter Redmond was born as the war ended.

In December Albert Timms died and was buried in Cottisford Church on December 17th.

c.1919   Flora began writing again and her earnings helped send Winifred and Basil to schools in Haslemere and Petersfield.

Flora answered an advertisement in the *Daily News* about a writing course offered by the Practical Correspondence College in London. As a result of taking the course she began submitting her work to the *Catholic Fireside*.

1920   Flora rewrote *The Leper* which was republished in *The Literary Monthly*.

Early 1921   Flora began to write a series of nature articles for the *Catholic Fireside*. The first of a series of 12 articles set in the New Forest was published in January 1st.

1921   *Bog Myrtle and Peat*, Flora's slim paperback of her poetry, was published, dedicated to Dr Ronald Macfie. It was not very successful and Flora became depressed.

1922   The style of the nature articles in the *Catholic Fireside* changed to become less fictional and more focused on nature. They were retitled *The Peverel Papers*, after her nickname for Weaver's Down,

Liphook. Over the next six years 72 *Peverel Papers* were written. Flora received letters praising her work, especially her sketches of country life, which gradually encouraged her to write about her childhood.

1923   Peter began school, giving Flora more time to write.

She initiated *The Fireside Reading Circle* for the *Catholic Fireside*. She wrote literary essays for the magazine on authors such as Dickens, George Eliot and the Brontes and more general studies on short stories, novels etc. She judged writing competitions for the Circle and through that became friendly with one competitor, Mildred Humble Smith.

*c.*1924   Flora's younger sister Ethel Elizabeth Timms (known as Betty), who also worked in the post office, won literary competitions.

*c.*1925   Flora joined the *Antiquarian and Field Society* attached to Haslemere Museum.

1925   Flora wrote a guidebook to Liphook.

Around this time her *Peverel Papers* began to include features on some of the characters she had known in her childhood such as Queenie and Old Sally.

Flora ended the *Fireside Reading Circle* in the *Catholic Fireside*. She and Mildred Humble-Smith instead founded *The Peverel Society*, with Lady Mary Sackville as their patron. The Society was advertised in the *Catholic Fireside*, offering writing courses.

Flora answered an advertisement in the *Literary Journal* to ghost-write for a big-game hunter, and her work was published in *The Scottish Field*, *Chamber's Journal* and various African papers.

1926   The Thompson's bought a house at Grigg's Green on the outskirts of Liphook.

Basil went to Australia, accompanied by Winifred's fiancé, initially to visit Flora's brother Frank who had emigrated to Queensland. Winifred's engagement did not survive.

Winifred worked at the Liphook Post Office telephone exchange. Flora's sister Betty often came to stay at Liphook. She had a book of children's stories published, *The Little Grey Men of the Moor*. Mildred Humble-Smith also had a children's book published, *Girls of Chiltern Towers*.

The first *Peverel Society Book of Verse* was published, which was favourably reviewed in *The Times Literary Supplement*.

1927   John Thompson was given the job of Postmaster in Dartmouth, Devon in August, to Flora's dismay, as she did not wish to leave Hampshire.

In December the last of the *Peverel Papers* was published.

1928   Flora, Winifred and Peter were able to stay at Woolmer Cottage while John house-hunted in Dartmouth. They did not move until the autumn.

Their new home, The Outlook, was in the Above Town area, approached by steep steps, with wonderful views.

John bought a small motor boat, *Sea Mew*, which he and Peter often took out to sea.

Basil had abandoned sheep farming in Australia and returned to try engineering.

Flora had no further connection with the *Catholic Fireside* and instead wrote more short stories, which do not appear to have been published.

She continued to spend much time on the Peverel Society.

1931   Flora's friend Dr Ronald Macfie, who had given her so much encouragement, died aged sixty six. Flora was very sad, writing his name on the flyleaf of a book with the quotation for Shakespeare's *Antony and Cleopatra*: "The bright day is done and we are for the dark."

1933   Flora's mother Emma Timms died aged eighty at Hethe, where she was living with one of Flora's sisters.

1935   John Thompson retired. He now appreciated Flora's writing and had built a writing room for her in their garden.

Flora began collecting together her memories about her childhood, writing verses of singing games in an empty diary.

Basil was working as an engineer on ships sailing between North and South America.

Winifred became a nurse.

Peter was apprenticed as a ship's engineer at Philip's shipyard.

1936   Flora sent a story, *The Tail-less Fox*, written in Liphook and set in a poor cottage, to *The Lady*, and it was published in December.

Flora realised that there was scope for more writing about her childhood.

1937   In April Flora's essay on *Old Queenie*, the lacemaker from Juniper Hill, was published in *The Lady*.

In August another essay entitled *An Oxfordshire Hamlet in the Eighties* was published in *The National Review*.

Flora began work in earnest on *Lark Rise*.

Basil, an engineer with the Prince Line between New York and Buenos Aires, married Dora Wallace in America.

1938
Basil brought Dora to visit his family.

May Day in the Eighties was published in the spring issue of *The National Review.*

Flora sent the completed text of *Lark Rise* to Oxford University Press. She was encouraged to extend the essays into a full length book by Sir Humphrey Milford, Published to the University. His deputy Geoffrey Cumberlege became her editor, and gave her continuing encouragement. The book had to be published as autobiography as the Press did not publish fiction.

In September illustrator Lynton Lamb stayed in Brackley and did ten pen and ink illustrations for Lark Rise.

1939
In March *Lark Rise* was published, widely reviewed in such magazines as *Country Life, The Sunday Times, The Times Literary Supplement.*

Her fame reached Oxfordshire, and she was delighted and amused when her family told her that Lady Bicester of Tusmore Park liked the book.

Flora worked on *Over to Candleford.*

In September war was declared. Winifred only just managed to get home from Switzerland before hostilities commenced.

Basil and his family had settled in Australia.

Peter worked till late each evening in the shipyard and then joined the Merchant Navy.

Flora was distracted from her work by making black-out curtains from old camping blankets.

John's war contribution was to become an ARP air raid warden. Flora had to take telephone messages when he was out. He spent his spare time fishing.

Flora and Mildred Humble-Smith discussed disbanding the Peverel Society for the duration of the war, but let it continue a little longer.

Flora continued working on *Over to Candleford*, but found it a great struggle. She even offered to return her advance to Oxford University Press, but Geoffrey Cumberlege urged her to continue.

1940
In March the Thompsons decided they were too vulnerable to bombing in Dartmouth, made a target by its Royal Naval College, harbour and shipyards. They found a cottage built on a hillside in Brixham called *Lauriston*, similar to one she describes in *Dashpers*. It was large enough for them to turn the spare room into a study for Flora.

John began to sell antiques on commission.

In June France fell to the Germans and the French coast was occupied. This led to air attacks along the Devon coast.

1941   The proofs of *Over to Candleford* were completed.

On 16th September the Thompsons received a telegram to say that Peter's ship, *The Jedmoor*, had been torpedoed, leaving only six survivors. Peter had died.

Flora, who was devastated by her son's death wrote to Geoffrey Cumberlege: "He was our youngest, a latecomer and tenderly loved. That there are thousands of mothers and wives suffering as I am only seems to make it harder to bear." (Harry Ransom)

Mildred Humble-Smith had also lost a son at sea, and neither of them had the heart to continue the Peverel Society, which was disbanded.

Despite her grief, Flora continued to work on her novel *Dashpers*, about a house and its inhabitants.

She contracted pneumonia during the winter and had to spend several weeks in bed.

1942   Flora had renewed strength to begin writing in the spring, but Dashpers was left to one side and she began *Candleford Green*. Writing was far from easy because of wartime conditions—there were many raids on Dartmouth and Brixham and Flora often had to retreat into her Morrison air raid shelter with her typescript.

1943   *Candleford Green* was published and was well received.

Geoffrey Cumberlege asked what she would like to offer next for publication. When she sent what she had written of *Dashpers* however, his comment was "I like everything you write, but I do not think this shows you at your happiest."

Flora instead sent him *The Peverel Papers* she had written for *The Catholic Fireside*, which were much more favourably received: "*The Peverel Papers* are full of good things . . . I can tell you here and now that we shall be delighted to publish it. (Harry Ransom) However, *The Peverel Papers* were not to be published until long after Flora's death.

Flora began a lengthy correspondence with her nephew Leslie, son of her sister Annie, who had written to say how much he appreciated the book.

Flora was still not well.

1944   Oxford University Press were planning to publish Flora's three books as a trilogy, *Lark Rise to Candleford*. The wood engraver Julie Neild was asked to do the illustrations. although wartime conditions prevented her from visiting Juniper Hill, she asked for much information from Flora to make her drawings as accurate as possible.

The introduction to the trilogy was written by the noted country writer H.J.Massingham who had already written appreciatively of Flora's work.

Flora was working on *Heatherley*, about her life at Grayshott, but it was never submitted for publication.

1945   In February Flora was ill with heart problems and depressed not to be able to go for walks when spring brought better weather. She commented wryly: "What a bore it is to get old and ill." (Letter in private collection quoted by Gillian Lindsay).

In March Flora received her advance copies of *Lark Rise to Candleford*, immediately signing the first one and returning it to Geoffrey Cumberlege.

The trilogy was published on 12th April. The edition of 5000 copies was sold out in advance.

The Second World War ended in Europe in May, making travel easier. Flora's nephew Leslie came to stay and was taken fishing by John. Flora's sister Betty often visited.

Basil and his wife, settled in Australia, now had three children.

Flora began to write another book, entitled *These Too Were Victorians*, which was to be published as *Still Glides the Stream*.

A Guild edition of *Lark Rise* was published, one third of which was sold to Australia and the Commonwealth.

1946   Flora was ill in the spring, suffering from angina. She was cheered and honoured on reading in *The Periodical*, produced by Oxford University Press, that the Publisher Sir Humphrey Milford considered that the two most important books he had published during his 22 years at the Press were A.J.Toynbee's *Study on History* and Flora Thompson's *Lark Rise to Candleford*.

In the summer John sold his boat *Sea Mew*, feeling he was too old to go out in it on his own.

Winifred came to stay for two weeks, enabling John to take a short holiday while she looked after Flora.

In August Flora completed *These Too Were Victorians*, retitled *Still Glides the Stream* before publication, which was probably based on Stoke Lyne or Hethe, or a mixture of the two. It was illustrated by Lynton Lamb.

In November the Reprint Society decided to publish 15,000 copies of *Lark Rise to Candleford*, offering royalties of about £1800 for Flora.

John was earning extra money buying and renting property and Flora bought 32 Bolton Street, Brixham, a double fronted house once used as a hotel, which was kept as an investment.

Leslie Castle bought a ticket for the Irish Sweep on Flora's behalf —she drew the favourite and sold part of the ticket for £250 so that she made a profit even when the horse only came in fourth. She sent £100 to Leslie.

On Armistice Day in November Flora laid a poppy wreath in memory of Peter at the Dartmouth war memorial. Leslie laid one for Edwin at Cottisford.

Flora was ill again over Christmas.

1947	Throughout the winter she worked on correcting the proofs of *Still Glides the Stream* and wrote an article about herself for *Readers News* as the Readers' Union were publishing an edition of *Lark Rise*. In May Flora seemed better and on 21st May John felt able to leave her for a day while he went out on business. She had an angina attack while he was out, followed by a heart attack that evening and died. Flora's funeral service was held at St Barnabas' Church in Dartmouth, followed by a cremation. Her ashes were buried at Longcross Cemetery, Dartmouth, with a gravestone in the shape of an open book which she shares with Peter. John Thompson was devastated by Flora's death. He stayed with friends in Bournemouth and then on the Isle of Wight. He sold their house *Lauriston*, moving to a smaller house in Brixham.
1948	*Still Glides the Stream* was published. John died on 13th July. Winifred became Flora's literary executor. She suggested the publication of *The Peverel Papers*, but although Geoffrey Cumberlege liked it, the project was not pursued. He was not interested in publishing *Gates of Eden*, her novel about a stonemason's daughter who runs away and falls in love with a married doctor poet. Around this time the biographer Margaret Lane travelled to Oxfordshire to research material for an article on Flora.
1949	Winifred was forced by ill-health to give up the nursing home in Cheltenham she had been running with two friends. The three of them retired to Bath.
1957	Margaret Lane published her essay about Flora Thompson in the *Cornhill magazine* in January.
1966	Winifred died.

The 90th anniversary of Flora's birth was marked by a performance of parts of *Lark Rise* in the grounds of Cottisford House. Evensong was held in Cottisford Church.

Lord David Cecil, Goldsmith's Professor of English at Oxford gave a lecture on *Lark Rise to Candleford* to an audience of 200 in the Rectory Barn, Cottisford.

1976   A small commemorative plaque was put on the wall of The End House, Juniper Hill, where Flora was brought up.

A literary lunch was held at The Anchor, Liphook with the guests of honour Geoffrey Cumberlege, Sir Hugh Casson and Margaret Lane. Anne Mallinson organised an exhibition about Flora's life and times at her Selborne Bookshop.

Sir Hugh Casson presented a short programme about Flora on BBC 2.

A *Lark Rise* festival was held at Shelswell Park.

1978   Keith Dewhurst's play *Lark Rise*, based on a day during the harvest, was performed at the National Theatre, London.

1979   Keith Dewhurst's *Candleford Green* was first performed at the National Theatre.

A Country Calendar was published by Oxford University Press with an essay by Margaret Lane on Flora's life, extracts from the *Peverel Papers*, some of Flora's poems and *Heatherley*.

1986   *The Peverel Papers*, edited by Julian Shuckburgh, was published by Century Hutchinson, featuring further extracts from Flora's nature writing.

1990   *Flora Thompson: The Story of the Lark Rise Writer*, the first full biography of Flora, written by Gillian Lindsay, was published by Robert Hale.

1997   On 21 May Ann Mallinson organised an event at Liphook to commemorate the 50th anniversary of Flora's death. John Owen Smith's play *'Flora's Peverel'* toured the Liphook area and his book *On the Trail of Flora Thompson beyond Candleford Green* was published.

APPENDIX 1

Money Owed by the Wallington Children to Local Tradesmen

Elizabeth Call, Shopkeeper of Piddington, for provisions	£18	0s	6¾d
Samuel Claridge, Haberdasher of Bicester for linen & hosiery	£14	0s	8d
Thomas Wood, Butcher of Ludgershall for butchers meat	£11	0s	1½d
Thomas Wallington, Butcher of Piddington, for butchers meat	£2	1s	11d
Aaron Foskett, Shoemaker of Grendon for shoes	£8	12s	2d
John George, Bicester for mercery and drapery	£7	6s	7d
William Jeacock, maltster of Marsh Gibbon for malt and beer	£12	0s	1d
John Scott, maltser of Marsh Gibbon for malt and beer	£1	7s	6d
William Golder, mealman of Blackthorn for flour and other goods	£9	1s	1d
John Jenkins, coalmerchant of Lower Heyford for coals	£7	8s	9d
William Parre, carpenter of Piddington for carpenter's work	£2	14s	5½d
John Jordan, shopkeeper of Piddington for provisions and clothing	£63	0s	0d
William Hawkins, the balance of an account for barley & a cow	£14	15s	6d
which together with other items, taxed, came to	£171	19s	10¾d

Money was also owed to Hannah Smith, schoolmistress of Islip, for board and education for the girls: £14 0s 6d for Clements (also known as Clementina), £3 7s 10d for Elizabeth and £29 17s 8d for Martha. Leonard owed £22 14s 6d to Abraham Chapman, schoolmaster of Islip and a further £8 11s for clothes to William Wharton, tailor and draper from Bicester.

APPENDIX 2

Inventory of the Fox Inn, Juniper Hill

Made in 1875 on the death of Thomas Harris

Tap room. Deal table, 1 elbow Windsor chair, eleven other ditto, 23 tumblers, butter cooler, steelyards and ball, 2 toasting forks, 15 champagne glasses, 5 smoothing irons, teapot, set of tea things, tea kettle, beer warmer, set of fire irons, 2 dozen plates, 12 meat dishes, 2 yellow ditto, 5 vegetable dishes, 2 basons, 6 cups and saucers, 3 corner cupboards, fender, 15 spitoons

Shop. About one quarter cut of bacon, about 10lb beef suet, deal counter, beam scales and 8 weights, part of a tin of lard, oak table with drawers, quantity of sweets, quarter of a gross of matches, 1 pair of candlesticks, pestal and mortar, 2 lamps, sugar nippers, night shade, pair of spurs, elbow and 5 chairs, mahogany table, writing desk, tea tray, 3 pewter measures, 1 funnel and 3 spirit measures.

Bakehouse. 2 washing trays and one tub, 2 flour bins, salting lead, 24 pint cups, 9 quart ditto, 9 quart jugs, 12 pint ditto, beam and flour scales and 2 weights, meat saw, spring balance and scale, 2 field bottles, 2 clothes baskets, 3 wooden water buckets, 2 galvanised ditto

Spirits, beer etc. 1 gallon of rum, 35 gallons of 9% beer, 18 gallons of mild

Hovel. About 21 bushels of potatoes, about 21 bushels seed potatoes, 3 bushels peas, 9 empty bags, 50 slates, ¼ bushel pig potatoes, 2 wheelbarrows, iron pig trough, chaff box and knife, bench, gate and sundry wood, 3 socket pipes, 2 stocks of bees, water butt and tap, about 120 bushels of potatoes, 2 shovels, washing bowl, 2 boilers, 4 iron saucepans, 1 tin ditto, 2 baking tins, strainer and Dutch oven, ½ bushel of flour, 3 beer cans, 2 hand saws , stone pig trough and 7 sacks

Bedroom No. 1. A four post bedstead and furniture, feather bed, flock mattress, feather bolster and 5 pillows, three blankets, counterpane, oak table, set of drawers. 4 volumes of books (The *Tablet*), 2 chairs, night commode, washstand and ware, large oak chest, 2 pieces of carpet, small lamp

Bedroom No. 2. French bedstead, flock mattress, straw ditto, feather bolster and pillow, 3 blankets, counterpane, round table and glass, large chest, clock in oak frame, broom, 3 chairs

Bedroom No. 3. 2 stump bedsteads, feather bed, bolster and 2 pillows, 2 flock mattresses, 3 blankets and counterpane, feather bed, straw mattress, 1 flock bolster, 1 feather ditto, counterpane, 2 blankets, dough kiver, 2 chairs

Bedroom No. 4. 4 post bedstead and furniture, feather bed, flock mattress, 3 blankets, counterpane, feather bolster and pillow, shut-up bedstead, painted chest of drawers, looking glass, clock, clothes line, 2 chairs, oak table, oak bureau, 5 pairs of sheets, 6 chamber towels, 6 tea cloths, 4 table cloths, 7 electro tea spoons, 3 metal spoons, 3 dozen black knives and forks, carver and fork, steel, 10 pillow cases

The Loft. 2 deal tables, 4 trestles, 4 skittles and ball, potato fork, 2 dung forks, 3 two-tine forks, spade and pickaxe, 2 iron bars, 12 besoms, cross cut saw, 9 stools

Coal House. Beam and scales, 3 × 56lb weights, 2 gates, pick and stoneaxe heads, about 10cwt of coal

Sow and six pigs. Iron pig trough

Value £96 10s 3d

Inventory of the Fringford Post Office and Forge, 1898

Blacksmith's shop

Pair of blacksmith's bellows, Tuyere iron, iron water trough, 9 pairs of tongs, 1 pair of pincers, poker, shovel, 3 copper bits, quantity of iron various, pair of old steel-yards, 3 new nudget chains, new chains, drilling machine. Quantity of staples and shut links, pair of scales, pair of compasses, sundries in window, iron vice, 2 old rasps, 2 old files, quantity of iron various, quantity of old bits, 8 spanners, quantity of old spanners, quantity of old horse shoes, 2 strings of washers, 11 door latches, quantity of hooks, nail tools, old castings, shoe iron, about 10 cwt of old shoes. 1 square rule, 2 old ditto, and 2 straight ditto, docking irons bull ringing irons 3 shoeing boxes and tools, anvil and block, quantity of screws 3 spanners, 9 pritchells, 9 hammers, 2 sledge hammers, quantity of scrap iron, anvil and wedge block.

Second Forge

12 pairs of tongs, shovel, poker, brush, pair of circular bellows, and tuyere iron, odd shoes, 2 screw hammers, 2 spanners, 2 braces and saw, 4 cold chisels, hand vice, 2 pairs of punches, pipe tongue, 2 rasps, 184 horse shoes, iron vice, small ditto, quantity of grate screens and taps, sundries in window, quantity of washers, tinman's tools, 12 files, 2 bull's feet parers, docking iron, tooth file, 3,600 horse nails, various sizes, quantity of nuts, scrap iron, 6 nail passers, small chisel, screw driver, spoke shaver, 1 drawing knife, mandrill and bulsters.

Store Room

10 wooden rakes, quantity of wood for stales, sundries, patterns etc., old ropes and old wire, scrap iron, 150 screws and bolts, old copper boiler, quantity of nails, nail box, 32 lbs clout nails, 3 gross of frost nails, 23 lbs screw bolts, quantity of common bolts, quantity of screw bolts various, 4 dozen rubbers, 1 bundle fork stales, 26 fork stales, broom paddle and mop stales, 2½ cwt of hoop iron, 6 new scythes, 2 sheets of tin, nest of drawers and contents, quantity of tow, 12 mowing machine knives, quantity of snap heads, sundry old nails and box, 15,000 horse nails, 2 shelves. About 2 tons of iron various, 5 galvanised sheets, 6 shovel handles, about 1¼ tons of coal, 6 spreaders, 12 × 4½ft stales, sundries.

Outside

A bay cob rising 4 years old, strong spring cart, lamps and rug, old boxes, quantity of straw, set of harness, stable tools, pig trough, hog tub and buckets, 60 gallon copper, quantity of blacksmith's coal, pig, pig trough, portable forge, sundries, old iron, ladder and 2 short ditto, 4 Scotch fir poles, 20 score of fir fagots, heap of manure, hard wood, 4 stocks of bees and patent hive, wheelbarrow, sack barrow, water tank and wheels, firewood, 2 boxes and contents, iron grease jack, 19 stamps and punches, old iron, quantity of bar and flat iron, 2 gross of roughing studs, tube expander, mandrill, 15 spring hooks, 18 galvanised ditto, 2 planes, padlock and key, 12 saw files, 5 hammer handles, 4 curry combs, 8 hoes, 7 wheat hoes, shoeing knife, engine jack, 5 iron bars, 2 cramps, hand saw, 2 bick irons, small mandrill, claw, 2 half pound files, 8 round files, 2 square files, quantities of files, 2 shoeing rasps, grindstone and frame, 5 stales. 6 shovel stales, 4 ash whippers, iron tooth draught rake, scythe and snathe and iron vices, 12 pairs of harness, drilling machine, 2 ratchet drills, quantity of screw bolts. 2 plough wheels, quantity of hame flats, quantity of handles, shoeing box and nails, 33 pair bits, sundries behind shoeing house door, 7 ft bar of steel, flat steel bar, sundry stocks and dies, garden tools, 4 augers, , shoeing stove and piping, iron mop box, drum firewood.

The Lane Shop.

Tyreing platform, quantity of coal, bellows and tuyere iron, wooden troughs and tools, anvil, bench and vice, cupboard, 3 tyreing dogs and hammer, 1 rake, stack of thorn faggots.

House Garden.

2 sacks of potatoes, garden produce

The Close.

Part of a rick of meadow hay, the continuous iron fencing

Stable.

Iron hay rack

Shoeing House.

Iron manger

Household Furniture

Bedroom No 1. A 4ft 6in stump bedstead, 2 cushions, flock bed, 3 flock pillows, feather bed and bolster, 4 blankets, coloured quilt, pair of sheets, 2 pieces of carpet and hearthrug, Windsor elbow chair, quantity of bed oakking, oak round table, 2 towel airers, dressing table, hair broom, carpet broom, rush seat, chair, clothes basket, blind roller, curtain rod and curtain.

No 2. A 4ft 3in wooden bedstead, double straw palliasse, feather bed bolster and pillow, 3 blankets and a coloured quilt, mahogany chest of drawers, painted wash-stand ware, towel airer, painted dressing table, swing glass, 3 pieces of carpet, mahogany night commode, 2 rush seated chairs, roller and muslin blinds.

No 3. Wooden bedstead, flock bed, feather bed, 2 pillows,, flock bolster, 3 blankets, quiilt,2 rush seated chairs, 3 pieces of carpet, corner washstand and ware, gal-vanised pan and glazed night pan, swing glass, roller blind.

No 4. Wooden bedstead, flock bed, 2 feather bolsters, 2 pillow, 3 blankets, 4 pieces of carpet, hearth rug, painted night commode. painted dressing table, swing glass, French bedstead, flock bed, 4 blankets, under blanket, pair of sheets, coloured quilt, 3 cane seated chairs, dressing table, painted chest of 5 drawers, painted washstand, mahogany swing glass, clock, roller blind.

Linen, Pair of twill sheets, 6 pairs of linen sheets, 7 pillow cases, 8 kitchen table cloths, 14 tea cloths, 10 table cloths, 8 old tea cloths, 11 round towels, 12 chamber towels, 6 towels, 6 knife cloths, 2 small table cloths.

Passage. Piece of Brussels carpet, 2 door mats, oak coffer. In cupboard: 4 dishes and 2 Vegetable dishes. chamber ware, high wire guard.

Parlour. Tapestry carpet, mahogany pembroke table, a two leaf oak table, pair decanters, fender and fire irons, coal hod, hassock, a two leaf oak table and cover, quantity of books. work table, 5 old trays, 2 coloured fruits, sundry ornaments, weather glass by Ortelli, 2 roller blinds, 3 cretonne curtains, mahogany easy chair, mahogany elbow chair, 6 Windsor chairs, clock, 2 Benzoline lamps, 6 stem glasses, 14 tumblers, 4 ale glasses, glass jug and dish 6 ports, 3 nip glasses, 1 stem glass, cruet stand, breakfast cruet, preserve dish, 2 glass salt cellars, 10 table, 2 dessert, 5 tea and 4 salt spoons. Set of 3 jugs, teapot, jug, glass sugar basin, glass butter dish.

Passage. cocoa fibre mat. A two leaf oak table and stool, a two leaf oak table with drawer. Timepiece, a 3-tier hanging shelf, paraffin lamp, hurricane lantern.

Kitchen. Dust pan, brush, shovel, 2 brushes, hair broom, fender, fire irons, iron saucepan, iron kettle, pieces of cocoa matting, 2 elbow wheelback Windsor chairs, oak stand table, a two leaf deal table with drawer, 5 and 1 elbow Windsor chairs. painted corner cupboard, a 30 hour clock in oak case, mahogany and oak bureau, paraffin lamp, roller blind, 2 iron curtain rods and green curtains. Iron curtain rod and pair of damask curtains, 7 old irons, 50 pieces of Cashmere soap, meat saw, wood spoon etc., 5 small lamps, quantity of knives, forks and spoons, 2 block tin teapots, blue and white teaware, sundry ware, 15 tea spoons, 6 spoons, shaving glass, boot jack, brass jack.

Pantry. 39 packets of cashmere soap, wine cask, 2 brown ware jars, 3 jars, jar of ketchup, 4 jars, 2 beer cans, perforated safe, 2 tins of lard, 2 baking tins, sundry ware etc., copper boiler, redware pan, three pewter plates, 2 oil tins and contents 2 barrel stills, wire egg basket.

Wash House. Salting lead and stand, copper kettle, hand bowl, wooden bowl, dinner ware, 2 pewter plates, tin bowl, deal table, clothes basket, coal hod, fish kettle, 3 iron saucepans, 2 copper boilers, 2 stools, 1½ sacks of white oats, Bradford's mangle, boot brushes etc. 4 wet hams, quantity wet bacon.

	£163 2s 9d
Add half share of stamp	5s 0d
	£163 7s 9d

Valued by the undersigned at the sum on One hundred and sixty three pounds seven shillings, and ninepence inclusive of half share of stamp

F.D.Holiday
Valuer, Bicester

INDEX

Names in small capitals are those invented by Flora Thompson for her characters and places. Numbers in bold indicate illustrations.